At Issue

Managing America's Forests

Stuart A. Kallen, *Book Editor*

Bruce Glassman, *Vice President*
Bonnie Szumski, *Publisher*
Helen Cothran, *Managing Editor*

GREENHAVEN PRESS
An imprint of Thomson Gale, a part of The Thomson Corporation

THOMSON
GALE

Detroit • New York • San Francisco • San Diego • New Haven, Conn.
Waterville, Maine • London • Munich

For more information, contact
Greenhaven Press
27500 Drake Rd.
Farmington Hills, MI 48331-3535
Or you can visit our Internet site at http://www.gale.com

LIBRARY OF CONGRESS CATALOGING-IN-PUBLICATION DATA

Managing America's forests / Stuart A. Kallen, book editor.
p. cm. — (At issue)
Includes bibliographical references and index.
ISBN 0-7377-2731-4 (lib. : alk. paper) — ISBN 0-7377-2732-2 (pbk. : alk. paper)
1. Forest management—United States. 2. Forests and forestry—Environmental aspects—United States. I. Kallen, Stuart A., 1955– . II. At issue (San Diego, Calif.)
SD143.M336 2005
333.75'0973—dc22 2004059929

Printed in the United States of America

Contents

Introduction

America's forests and trees represent many things to many people. Environmentalists and backpackers see woodlands as magnificent cathedrals of nature filled with ancient trees that have been growing for generations. Rural residents living near national forests see these same trees as a potential source of jobs for their family members who are loggers, mill workers, and wood finishers. Off-road vehicle (ORV) enthusiasts see a place where they can test their driving skills and courage zipping down a trail as fast as possible. Biologists may be searching for rare or endangered species or a microbe that might someday cure a fatal disease. Executives of a multinational paper products corporation may view the forest as a source of timber that can be profitably logged to make shopping bags, newsprint, and toilet paper.

In a nation of 290 million people, it seems that almost everyone has a different opinion of how the trees and the forests should be managed. And the debate seems nearly impossible to resolve when federal forest management regulations can fundamentally shift depending on whether the president favors industry or stronger environmental regulations. For example, when Democrat Bill Clinton was president, he had the backing of many national environmental organizations. Clinton set aside huge areas of forest for protection under the Roadless Area Conservation Rule, enacted in early January 2001, days before he left office. The rule banned road building, logging, mining, and other commercial development in 58.5 million acres of America's national forests, an area equal to 2 percent of all lands in the United States and 31 percent of all Forest Service lands.

Rural residents and others who were most affected by the roadless rule were outraged at what they called a 58-million-acre landgrab. Not only did the rule prevent logging and the jobs it creates but it also prevented off-road vehicle users from having access to huge swaths of public lands. Representative George Radanovich (R-CA) summed up their feelings: "To say that the public cannot access their land unless the federal government gives them permission is in fundamental opposition to the freedoms on which our country was founded."

When George W. Bush became president only weeks after the Clinton's roadless rule went into effect, he immediately took steps to reverse the policy, dropping the Clinton provisions in the summer of 2004. Many environmentalists were disappointed. Environmental attorney Simeon Herskovits told the *Los Angeles Times*, that the Bush decision "is largely about removing any roadblocks that may have been erected in the last couple of decades to oil and gas development, timber harvesting, [and] hard-rock mining."

In this and so many other debates about forest management, the Forest Service is caught between the demands of environmentalists, ORV riders, forest workers, industry executives, and others. The laws governing national forests say that the woodlands should be managed for what is called "multiple use." This term is all-encompassing, including logging, mining, energy production, hiking, camping, motorized recreation, and wildlife and water protection. Overriding all these mandates, laws to protect endangered species and clean water must also be enforced. The dilemma posed by multiple use management is explained by scholar Donald W. Floyd in the book *Forest of Discord:*

> Using the national forests and the public lands for a variety of purposes is not an unreasonable goal, but some uses are incompatible with others and cannot be achieved simultaneously or equally across a landscape. Multiple use has thus become an engine of conflict that pits one interest group against another and denies land managers a clear mandate.

The conflicting directives of the Forest Service come into sharper focus during times of crises, such as when millions of acres are burned by wildfires. These conflagrations, aggravated since the 1980s by years of prolonged drought in the West, cause billions of dollars of property damage and have killed dozens of firefighters and local residents. In 2003, in response to several major wildfires, President Bush signed the Healthy Forests Restoration Act. The law is meant to expedite forest-thinning projects that would reduce fuel buildup. As Bush said when he signed the bill into law:

> We need to thin [the forests]. . . . We need to make

> our forests healthy by using some common sense. . . . We need to understand, if you let kindling build up and there's a lightning strike, you're going to get yourself a big fire.

The law suspends environmental protection in the form of the Endangered Species Act, the National Environmental Policy Act, and the National Forest Management Act in forests that have suffered wildfires. It also eliminates lawsuits, appeals, and judicial review of logging operations in areas that have been burned.

Environmentalists, however, say that thinning will actually increase the fire danger, as a 2002 Sierra Club report argues:

> [Logging] operations are likely to remove the [tree] trunks for lumber while leaving behind mountains of slash that can ignite into a raging bonfire, or they leave behind clearcuts littered with tinder across which wildfires can race and grow. . . . [When] thinning is used as a method of fire prevention, the dense and flammable brush that leads to intense fires is not sufficiently removed.

The debate continues with homeowners, environmentalists, loggers, foresters, politicians, and scientists offering often competing visions of forest management. When one group is successful in implementing their ideas into law, the others file lawsuits to stop the program from going forward. Heated accusations, name-calling, and finger-pointing abound in news stories, editorials, and protest marches. As Floyd writes:

> Conflicts over resources have sparked wars and armed conflicts around the world. In the United States we have left the battlefield for the courtroom—and the court of public opinion—but the conflicts are no less impassioned just because the adversaries advance their cause by brandishing laws and regulations instead of swords and rifles.

Many aspects of this ongoing debate are presented in *At Issue: Managing America's Forests*. There is little doubt that the arguments will continue into the foreseeable future. As long as some see forests as sources of wood and paper products while others see pristine wilderness, competing visions will result in politically charged debates.

1

Managers Need to Address the Four Major Threats to America's Forests

Dale Bosworth

Dale Bosworth is a forester who worked in the national forests of Montana, Utah, and Idaho before becoming the chief of the Forest Service in 2001.

National forests face major threats that could have grave consequences for the health of American woodlands. Forest managers need to solve the serious problems of fire control, invasive species, loss of open spaces to development, and unmanaged recreation destroying wildlife and land. The Forest Service needs to open a national debate about how to address each of those threats to America's forests and must involve the public in its decision making.

For a number of years, Americans have faced growing threats to our quality of life. At the Forest Service, we've tried to promote a national dialogue about those threats. At our recent National Leadership Team meeting [in 2003], we talked about four major threats: fire and fuels; unwanted invasive species; loss of open space; and the impacts of unmanaged recreation, particularly the unmanaged use of off-highway vehicles. Today, I want to say a little about those four threats. . . .

Dale Bosworth, "We Need a New National Debate," www.fs.fed.us, July 17, 2003.

We all have strong opinions about how to manage the land, and with those opinions naturally comes debate. I think having a debate is good and necessary, particularly when it comes to public lands. We need to hash out any conflicts we might have so we can come to agreement about how to manage these lands.

> *"We can remove some of the trees and lower the risk of fire danger; or we can do nothing and watch them burn."*

So debate isn't the problem. The problem is the direction the debate has taken in recent years. I think the debate focuses on the wrong issues for the beginning of the 21st century. Times have changed; we should be focusing on four great threats—fire and fuels, unwanted invasive species, loss of open space, and unmanaged recreation. I'll say a little about each.

Fire and Fuels

One great threat is fire and fuels. In two of the last three years, we've had some of our biggest fire seasons since the 1950s. Four states had record fires last year [2002], and a fifth came close. This year, parts of the West are again being threatened. For example, the Aspen Fire near Tucson, Arizona, . . . burned more than 80,000 acres and destroyed hundreds of homes [in 2003].

The underlying issue is that so many of our forests have become overgrown and unhealthy. I don't want to oversimplify—many of America's forests are healthy, and some forest types were always dense. Big fires naturally occur in these forests, but not very often. But some ecosystems are not adapted to big stand replacement fires. Instead, they are adapted to low fires that used to come quite often. Some fire-adapted forests had fires as often as every few years.

Then came decades of fire exclusion and overgrazing in some areas, resulting in fewer low-intensity fires. A wetter climate in the West also favored woody plant growth, and in the last decade we've had declining timber harvest on most national forests. As a result of all these things, brush and small trees have built up in many areas. Just to give you some idea, in the Southwest—Arizona and New Mexico—annual growth is enough to cover a football field 1 mile high with solid wood, even after losses from mortality. Recent removals have been only about 10 percent of this.

Today, there's a drought in many of these overgrown forests, and fires no longer stay low to the ground. Instead, they tend to burn up through the undergrowth and into the tree crowns. The entire forest might burn up. Both people and ecosystems are at risk.

On the national forests alone, 73 million acres adapted to frequent fire are at risk from wildland fires that could compromise human safety and ecosystem health. That's an area about half again the size of South Dakota—a pretty big chunk of ground. And it's not just on the national forests—it's all across America. In fact, some 397 million acres fall into the same category of moderate to severe fire risk—about a fifth of the contiguous United States. National forest land makes up only a fraction of that.

Americans must decide: We can remove some of the trees and lower the risk of fire danger; or we can do nothing and watch them burn. I think the choice is obvious: In a good part of the country—where fire-adapted forests are overgrown—we must return forests to something more like the way they were historically, then get fire back into the ecosystem when it's safe.

I mentioned the Aspen Fire near Tucson in Arizona. It's a good example of both the challenges and the opportunities we face. Before the fire came through, we'd done some fuels treatments in some areas. Some of them worked to make the fire less severe, and some didn't. But after the fire started, we did some burning out to protect homes in much the same way we do controlled burns for fuels management. In many of those burnouts, the fire did what we hoped. It dropped to the ground, and homes were saved. That just goes to show that our treatments can work.

Unwanted Invasive Species

The second great threat is the spread of unwanted invasive species. These include not just plants, but also animals and even disease-causing pathogens—things like West Nile virus or monkeypox. They are species that evolved in one place and wound up in another, where the ecological controls they evolved with are missing. They take advantage of their new surroundings to crowd out or kill off native species. In the process, they might alter key ecological processes, such as hydrology or fire return intervals.

Unwanted invasive plants alone give you some idea of the scope of the problem. Nationwide, invasive plants now cover an area larger than the entire Northeast, from Pennsylvania to Maine. Each year, they gobble up an area larger than the state of Delaware. Every region has its own major problem with invasive species—gypsy moth in the Northeast, kudzu vine in the South, white pine blister rust in the West. All invasives combined cost Americans about $138 billion per year in total economic damages and associated control costs.

The ecological costs are even worse. The Nature Conservancy and NatureServe sponsored a recent [2002] study on the major causes of biodiversity loss in the United States. The study found that invasives have contributed to the decline of almost half of all imperiled species.

So this is a huge issue for the Forest Service, and it should be for all Americans. Public lands—especially federal lands—have become a last refuge for endangered species—some of the last places where they can find the habitat they need to survive. If invasives take over, imperiled animals and plants will have nowhere else to go. We are losing our precious heritage.

Loss of Open Space

That brings me to the third great threat—loss of open space through urban development. Every day, we lose about 4,000 acres of open space to development. That's almost 3 acres per minute, and the rate of conversion is getting faster all the time.

Our population is growing, especially in counties with national forests, which are huge retirement magnets. The pressures are especially obvious in the East, where about 4 out of 10 Americans live and where almost half of the nation's 20 largest cities are located. . . . I'm sure you've noticed the pressures on open space—the heavy use, the summer homes, the growing wildland/urban interface.

The South is seeing similar land use changes. Last year [2002], we completed a major multiyear assessment of southern forest resources, and we found that urban land uses are rapidly expanding. We also found that rising urban use is altering forest structure in large parts of the South while limiting management options, such as prescribed fire.

Maybe the biggest threat is to wildlife. Urbanization eats away at forest interior habitat by eliminating large blocks of unfragmented forest. America is losing valuable corridors needed to connect parts of the national forests with other large undisturbed tracts of land. Animals like marten, bear, or cougar need large, relatively undisturbed forests to survive. Many birds also need forest interior habitat.

We're also losing rangeland habitat in the West. Developers often target the bottomlands adjacent to federal land. Millions of acres of open range have been converted to ranchettes, condominiums, and other developed land. That means we're losing the ecological integrity of the land as a whole. Elk, for example, depend on lower slopes and bottomland for winter range. Without it, they won't survive, no matter how good the habitat is on adjacent public land.

Unmanaged Outdoor Recreation

The fourth great threat comes from unmanaged outdoor recreation. In my years with the Forest Service, I have seen a tremendous growth in the amount of recreation on the national forests. I think that's great. It gives people a stake in the land and a stronger sense of place.

The issue is this: Back when we had light recreational use, we didn't need to manage it so much; but now that it's heavier, we do. There are still uses like blueberry picking that we don't need to manage much. But if every blueberry was picked, we would need to manage it more. At one time, we didn't need to manage mushroom picking much, but now we do in some areas.

> *"Every day, we lose about 4,000 acres of open space to development."*

At one time, we didn't much manage the use of horses or vehicles, either. But horseback riding has reached levels that are causing serious concern in some parts of the South and East. Nationwide, something similar goes for off-highway vehicles [OHVs].

OHVs are a great way to experience the outdoors, and only a tiny fraction of the users leave lasting traces by going cross-country. But the number of OHV users has just exploded in recent years. Even a tiny percentage of impact from all those millions of OHV users is still a lot of impact.

> *"The number of OHV users has just exploded in recent years. Even a tiny percentage of impact from all those millions of OHV users is still a lot of impact."*

Each year, the national forests and grasslands get hundreds of miles of unauthorized roads and trails due to repeated cross-country use. We're seeing more and more erosion, water degradation, and habitat destruction. We're seeing more and more conflicts between users. We're seeing more damage to cultural sites and more violation of sites sacred to American Indians. And those are just some of the impacts. We've got to get a handle on that.

Finding Solutions

Those are the four great threats we face today—fire and fuels, invasive species, loss of open space, and unmanaged outdoor recreation. I don't mean to suggest that these are the only land management challenges we face or that they are entirely new. In fact, [some environmental groups have] been addressing them for years. . . . Let me just briefly outline some of what we've been doing:

• *Fire and fuels:* The National Fire Plan and the Healthy Forests Initiative [signed by President Bush in 2004] are working. With the help of the western governors and other partners, we have agreed on the need to focus our treatments on the areas most at risk, such as long-needle pine ecosystems near communities and in municipal watersheds. In fiscal year 2002, the federal agencies together treated about 2.26 million acres, a big increase over treatment levels a decade ago.

• *Invasive species:* When it comes to invasive species, I think we can all agree that prevention and control work best, but only if they are done across ownerships on a landscape level. The Forest Service has some good partnership programs with the states, such as "Slow-the-Spread" for gypsy moth in the Northeast.

• *Urbanization:* A good way to conserve open space is to keep ranches and working forests in operation, and the Forest Service has some programs for that. We've got conservation easements through the states so that willing landowners can keep their lands forested. . . . We've also got forage reserves that ranchers can use to give their grazing allotments a rest. Through programs like these, we can work together across the landscape to keep the land whole.

• *Unmanaged recreation:* We encourage local programs to keep OHV use on designated roads and trails. National user groups such as the Blue Ribbon Coalition have pledged to work with us to promote responsible OHV use. The focus is on improving our own travel management through better inventory and maps, more public involvement, clear standards and guides in forest plans, clearer signage, better communication, and local partnerships for road maintenance.

So we are making progress, but there's still a long way to go. For example, although we've picked up the pace of our forest health treatments, they are still far below the levels called for in a strategy we prepared in 2000. Are we still falling behind on federal lands? And what about state and private lands? Such questions don't have easy answers. In fact, we're going to need to resolve them through a vigorous national debate.

Diversions

So what's stopping us? Unfortunately, we're distracted by other issues. Too many folks are stuck in the past, still fighting the same old battles from 20 or 30 years ago. We're too focused on logging, some people tell us; we're too focused on building new roads. But it's just not true:

• Today, the national forests produce less than 2 billion board feet of timber per year. That's less than 15 percent of what we produced 15 or 20 years ago. In terms of sheer weight, Americans produce more woody yard waste than national forest timber.

• In the last 5 years, for every mile we added to the forest road system, the Forest Service decommissioned 14 miles of road. Our road system is not growing, it's shrinking.

The fact is, our management is not what it was 15 or 20 years ago. Instead of mitigating damage from *outputs*, we now capitalize on activities for generating *outcomes*. That includes using vegetation removal as a tool for restoring healthy, resilient forest ecosystems. That's why the debate today—focusing on limits to diameter size of the trees we remove—misses the mark. Some people contend that forests are unsustainable if we remove any trees at all over a certain diameter size. To my knowledge, there is no science to support that.

In my view, the way to manage for clean air, clean water, and healthy habitat is to focus on what we leave on the land, not on what we take away. On a landscape scale, the number and size of the trees we remove doesn't matter. What matters is what we leave on the land to achieve healthy landscape conditions. The goal is to meet the desired future condition. . . .

In closing, I think it's time we focused on what's really at risk. I'm not saying we have all the answers—we don't. In fact, we need an open, productive debate on what to do about each of these threats. We must continue to welcome upfront public involvement in our decision making and constructive criticism of everything we do. But beyond that, we've got to stop debating the past and start looking to the future. It's time to move on.

2

The Forest Service Is No Longer Capable of Managing National Forests

Roger A. Sedjo

Roger A. Sedjo is a senior fellow and director of the Forest Economics and Policy Program at Resources for the Future in Washington, D.C. He has served as a member of the U.S. Department of Agriculture's Committee of Scientists and is the author of the book A Vision for the Forest Service.

When the Forest Service was created in the early twentieth century, its mandate was simple: to ensure that the people of the United States would never run out of timber for building, manufacturing, and paper production. Since the 1970s, however, Congress has given several different, and often conflicting, mandates to the Forest Service—from protecting endangered species to preserving wilderness and watersheds. With the public deeply divided over issues such as environmental preservation and logging, the end result has been to politicize the Forest Service to the point that it can no longer manage America's national forests. It is time for Congress to disband the Forest Service or integrate it with the Bureau of Land Management.

The Forest Service is in deep trouble. Its mission is not unique, it is deeply politicized, and it lacks a serious supporting constituency. Historically, the agency's mission has been fairly well

Roger A. Sedjo, "Does the Forest Service Have a Future?" *Regulation*, vol. 23, Spring 2000, p. 51.

defined. The 1897 Organic Act [the law that established the Forest Service] gave three purposes to the forest reserves:

- Preserve and protect the forest within the reservation.
- Secure favorable conditions of water flows.
- Furnish a continuous supply of timber for the use and necessities of the people of the United States.

Before World War II, timber harvests were modest but in the postwar boom, the harvests increased markedly. Gradually, the Forest Service's mission was expanded to include recreation, wildlife habitat, and wilderness—and the conflicts have increased. With the advent of the [1973] Endangered Species Act (ESA), and its increasingly interventionist interpretations by the courts, the agency's focus has shifted dramatically from timber to other outputs, especially biodiversity. [Since 1991] timber harvests have plummeted, while recreation, wildlife habitat, and wilderness have increased markedly.

> *"It seems that nobody is happy with the Forest Service."*

The most recent comprehensive forest legislation, the National Forest Management Act (NFMA) of 1976, mandates that the Forest Service provide for "multiple use and sustained yield of the products and services obtained therefrom, . . . and, in particular include coordination of outdoor recreation, range, timber, watershed, wildlife and fish, and wilderness."

The legislation appears clear and unequivocal. The Forest Service must provide for the sustainable production of the seven products and services explicitly mentioned. The outputs are clearly identified, as is the requirement that they be produced on a sustainable basis. So, why does the Forest Service need "a clarification of mission"?

The problem is that court rulings about ESA and the regulations written to implement NFMA give biological and ecological considerations priority over other goals. The regulations developed to implement NFMA, for example, require the Forest Service to ensure the widespread maintenance of viable plant and animal populations. The result has been a serious disconnection between the directives of the agency's statutory mandate and the nature of its activities and management. . . .

The Agency's History

In response to public concerns over water conditions and future timber supplies in the latter part of the 19th century, large areas of public lands were designated as part of the nation's "forest reserves," later to be called the National Forest System [NFS]. However, even in that early period, there were alternative perspectives and philosophies of the objectives of forest maintenance. The pragmatism of the conservationists, as represented by [first chief of the Forest Service Gifford] Pinchot, was reflected in their concept of the "wise use" of resources. The philosophy of wise resource use was pitted against the views of preservationists, such as [John] Muir and, perhaps [Henry David] Thoreau. The American people wanted water and future timber, but they were also concerned about preserving naturalness, wildness, and wilderness, which were, even then, recognized as part of the American heritage.

Although these two philosophies vied for dominance in that early period, the on-the-ground conflicts between them were small, largely because the Forest Service assumed primarily a custodial role. The public forest provided only modest amounts of timber, allowing preservation of the vast majority.

With the advent of World War II and in the subsequent postwar period, the national forests took on a new importance as a source of timber. They met the needs of the war period, subsequently produced substantial volumes of timber for the postwar housing boom, and continued high levels of output into the late 1980s.

Agency's Mandate Expanded

Environmentalists and others thought NFS's emphasis on timber was too great and should also include other forest outputs. A series of legislative acts (Multiple Use Sustained Yield Act of 1960, Resources Planning Act in 1974, and NFMA in 1976) instructed the Forest Service to produce multiple outputs, including timber, range, wildlife, recreation, water, and (less explicitly) wilderness. The "trick" was to produce these outputs jointly and to produce the appropriate mix to satisfy the various constituencies. In addition, the laws required that these outputs be produced in a sustainable manner. Given this general mandate, a forest-planning process was created that was intended to allow all of the interested parties to participate in management and output decisions. The assumption was that the planning process would provide a vehicle for the various interests to work out their differences and reach a consensus forest plan with a broadly acceptable mix of actions and outputs. Also, it was implicitly assumed that if a consensus on the forest plan were reached regarding the goals of forest management in a particular forest, Congress would provide the budget to implement those objectives.

> *"In recent decades, the Forest Service has truly been given a 'mission impossible.'"*

In the two and a half decades since NFMA enactment, little of what was envisaged has come to pass. Although the periodic resource assessment has been undertaken regularly, the planning process has largely been a failure. For example, it has not generated the desired consensus. In the first 125 forest management plans, there were about 1,200 appeals and over 100 subsequent lawsuits. Some appeals have been in process for almost a decade without resolution. Even when plans were approved, budgets were generally not forthcoming to allow faithful implementation. There is little connection between the budget that emerges from the congressional political process and provides funds on an aggregate programmatic basis and the various forest plans developed through the decentralized planning process created by NFMA.

No Longer an Elite Agency

Traditionally, the Forest Service had been viewed as an elite agency. This perspective emerged out of the ties between Pinchot and President Teddy Roosevelt. . . . Consistent with the positive view of progressivism and scientific management, the Forest Service was able to recruit the best and the brightest foresters trained in new European techniques. This was a new agency with a highly trained and committed professional staff. The view of professionalism was maintained for many years. Until the early 1990s, the chief of the Forest Service was still essentially a nonpolitical position drawn from the ranks of its senior professionals.

The Forest Service made the most of its positive image. In

the early 1960s, Herbert Kaufman wrote his famous book *The Forest Ranger,* in which the Forest Service was used as an example of how a large public government agency should function. He argued that, unique among large organizations, the Forest Service had been able to maintain its focus, its discipline, and its esprit de corps.

The high esteem in which the Forest Service was held was not limited to the public; it carried over to Congress, which gave it large budgets and autonomy. In his book *Public Lands Politics,* Paul Culhane argued that the Forest Service had successfully been able to maintain a high degree of autonomy as the various interest groups competed against one another. The groups he examined—timber interests, environmentalists, and recreationists—all provided the agency with constituencies that supported its budget requests and programs. In return, the Forest Service provided the outputs desired by each group. Because the interests were so diverse but relatively balanced, the Forest Service had decision-making autonomy: it could justify an action undesirable to one of the groups by arguing that it was necessary to pacify one of its other constituencies—which wanted even more. Furthermore, when the time for budget decisions arrived, these groups could still be relied on to support the various facets of the agency's budgets.

Today, few would view the Forest Service as an elite agency. Local users of national forest lands are highly disenchanted and discouraged. Recreationists, environmentalists, and timber users also voice major complaints. It seems that nobody is happy with the Forest Service. . . .

The Current Situation

The forest service's happy situation in earlier periods has seriously eroded over recent decades. I believe that the system has broken down because the fine balance among the various competing constituencies gradually disappeared. The battles among these groups—particularly the environmentalists and timber interests—compelled Congress to pass NFMA to try to restore order and the balance. However, that was not to be. The environmentalists have swept the field. The NFMA planning process provided a vehicle to challenge plans that were viewed as undesirable, even if a group did not participate in the planning deliberations. Additionally, a host of environmental laws and their evolving judicial interpretation forced both a reduction in harvest levels and a rethinking of policy. Timber harvest levels, which peaked in the late 1980s under the still-existing NFMA legislation, have since declined to less than one-quarter of their peak levels.

Whatever its past "sins," in recent decades, the Forest Service has truly been given a "mission impossible." It is being asked to reflect the will of the people when, in fact, we are deeply divided. There is no shared vision of the role of public forestlands. Attempts to "reinvent" the role of the Forest Service continue to be frustrated by a lack of consensus. Furthermore, attempts to formulate new legislation to impart better-defined implicit property rights to the contenders are going nowhere. . . .

Where Do We Go from Here?

Let us examine three potential candidates for a Forest Service mission and constituency: biological preservation, recreation, and local control.

Biological Preservation: Recently, a committee of scientists was assembled by the secretary of agriculture to "provide scientific and technical advice to the Secretary of Agriculture and the Chief of the Forest Service on Improvement that can be made in the NFS Land and Resource planning process." In its report, *Sustaining the People's Lands,* the committee decided to provide the mission statement that the Forest Service has lacked. Casting aside concerns about whether it is appropriate for the committee to dictate a mission for the agency, the committee boldly declared that the binding charge has been sustainability and recommended, in essence, that the Forest Service manage for ecological sustainability. . . .

Having asserted a mission for the Forest Service that Congress and the administration were reluctant to state, the committee then suggested ways in which this objective might be accomplished. The committee's report argued that sustainability was paramount and, in essence, the legislative multiple-use mandate should be replaced de facto by an alternative objective—that of maintaining what is essentially ecological sustainability.

In my view, such an approach is, in effect, an obituary for the Forest Service as we know it. In the absence of significant tangible outputs, it is doubtful that sufficient public support exists to generate serious budgets for a program focused primarily on maintaining ecological sustainability. Although many people may support such an approach in concept, it is doubtful that this support could develop into a constituency with the power to generate substantial and continuing budgets for these types of management activities. The services rendered through the activities would be difficult for the public to perceive on a regular basis, and the major direct financial beneficiaries would be the biologists and ecologists employed in the process.

Although major environmental groups support facets of an ecological mission, many of them oppose timber harvesting of any type, including that necessary to meet other objectives (e.g., wildlife habitat). Indeed, many favor an essentially hands-off approach to "management." Because of their persistent distrust of the motives of the Forest Service, it is doubtful that these groups would enthusiastically support the large budget necessary to manage ecological sustainability. The likely outcome would be the erosion of the agency's budget as custodial management and protection supplant active management.

"There is no shared vision of the role of public forestlands. Attempts to 'reinvent' the role of the Forest Service continue to be frustrated by a lack of consensus."

Recreation: Perhaps the major constituency that could emerge to lead in supporting the Forest Service is the recreationists. The National Forest System provides many types of outdoor recreation. Although recreational users are far from monolithic in their interests and the services desired from the agency, their numbers are large. Perhaps most intriguing is the possibility of generating a substantial portion of the budget for various forests from recreational user fees. Certainly, many forests have the potential to raise substantial funds from recreational user fees. Some forests near urban centers have demonstrated the ability to generate substantial amounts in user fees. However, such fees are often difficult and costly to collect. Nevertheless, it has been argued that for many national forests, the recreational benefits far exceed the timber and other traditional output benefits. If this is true, user fees could well provide major revenues for many, but surely not all, national forests. In this context, Forest Service budgets could be, in substantial part, financed from recreational receipts and supplemented by more modest allocations from Congress. Of course, such an approach would require that the agency have some control over the user fees it generates.

If funding were dependent on recreational use, there would be powerful incentives to provide the types of outputs desired by recreationists. Furthermore, the role of federal funding and the ability of a constituency to support the Forest Service budget in Congress become less important if the agency can cover a substantial portion of its costs with user fees. Finally, it should be noted that the various recreational uses may conflict, and recreational use could well lead to conflicts with other desired outputs and services, including biodiversity. Thus, although this approach appears to have much to commend it, there is certainly no guarantee that future conflicts between the various user groups can be avoided.

Local Control: A third option would be to move toward more localized input into the management of the national forests. . . . In Canada, after all, the respective provinces control the forests. Perhaps Congress should consider budgeting individual national forests or groups of national forests, in a manner akin to the separate budgeting of the national parks. This arrangement could allow management to be customized—to a degree not previously seen—to the needs and desires of the local people. Some combination of user fees and customized management could provide both for adequate funding and for the emergence of powerful local constituencies. This approach could allow a level of local participation that has not been experienced in decades. It should be noted, however, that many national environmental groups oppose this approach. Shifting power to the local community implies reducing the influence of national groups on local situations.

Nevertheless, [this] solution offers promise in that it addresses the budget and constituency challenges facing the Forest Service in a way other approaches do not. And local authority could judge the health of the forest and the desirability of various remedial approaches. A decentralized approach has substantial merit in "returning" much of the effective control of forest management to local people, who could then customize management to the needs of the region. In many cases, such an approach would also provide local communities with additional revenues for financial management and other local needs. . . .

Department of Natural Resources?

Perhaps the most fundamental issue is whether to retain a separate Forest Service at all. Arguments for the coordination of land management are now louder than ever and played a prominent role in the Committee of Scientists' Report.

The original rationale for a forest service focused on the desire to create an elite organization that had technocratic prowess and a degree of independence from the bureaucratic and political processes so that it could "do the right thing" based on its professional judgment. The Forest Service is no longer an elite organization. Although it still retains many highly trained and competent people, the Forest Service is no longer unique. In fact, it is probably more wracked with confusion than most agencies from the many years its mission has lacked clarity or has been highly ambiguous. It is also no longer insulated from the ravages of the bureaucratic process and crass politics. . . . The fine balance among constituencies, which Culhane saw as the core of the agency's ability to fend off crass political pressures, no longer exists. Furthermore, its ability to supply services to various constituencies is minimal. It is now beholden to a single group in society rather than to a host of groups.

Today, there may be a compelling reason to integrate federal land management agencies. Perhaps it is time to reconsider the proposals of the Carter administration, which called for a unified department of natural resources that would include the Forest Service. Perhaps it is time to merge the Forest Service and the Bureau of Land Management into one agency. Surely, the rationale for such integration becomes more compelling as the Forest Service loses both its unique mission and its unique ability to perform any mission in an outstanding manner.

3

Large-Scale Timber Harvesting Is Good for the Environment

Patrick Moore

Patrick Moore is one of the founders of the environmental organization Greenpeace. He left the group to found Greenspirit, which promotes large-scale logging, expanded nuclear energy production, and the widespread planting of genetically modified crops.

Millions of people throughout the world depend on wood for cheap paper products as well as for energy for cooking and heating. The demand for wood and paper products continues to grow even as environmental organizations try to ban all logging. The fact is that trees are a renewable resource that can be planted and harvested just like any farm crop. In order to wean society from polluting, nonrenewable resources such as oil, forest managers should plant as many trees as possible, even converting agricultural fields to tree farms. By harvesting trees for energy, people can slow global warming, reduce dependence on oil, and make life better for the world's poor.

I believe that trees are the answer to a lot of questions about our future. These include: How can we advance to a more sustainable economy based on renewable fuels and materials? How can we improve literacy and sanitation in developing countries while reversing deforestation and protecting wildlife

Patrick Moore, "Trees Are the Answer," Greenspirit, www.greenspirit.com, 2002.

at the same time? How can we pull carbon out of the atmosphere and reduce the amount of greenhouse gases emissions, carbon dioxide in particular? How can we increase the amount of land that will support a greater diversity of species? How can we help prevent soil erosion and provide clean air and water? How can we make this world more beautiful and green? The answer is, by growing more trees and then using more wood, both as a substitute for non-renewable fossil fuels and materials such as steel, concrete and plastic, and as paper products for printing, packaging and sanitation.

> *"To the best of our scientific knowledge, no species has become extinct in North America due to forestry."*

The forest industry stands accused of some very serious crimes against the environment. It is charged with the extinction of tens of thousands of species, the deforestation of vast areas of the Earth, and the total and irreversible destruction of the ecosystem. If I were one of the urban majority, and I thought the forest industry was causing the irreversible destruction of the environment I wouldn't care how many jobs it created or how many communities depended on it, I would be against it.

I have spent the last 15 years trying to understand the relationship between forestry and the environment, to separate fact from fiction, myth from reality. . . . This [article] is the synthesis of what I have learned. . . .

Achieving Sustainable Development

The term sustainable development was adopted [in the mid-1980s] to describe the challenge of taking the new environmental values [Greenpeace and other environmental groups] had popularized, and incorporating them into the traditional social and economic values that have always governed public policy and our daily behavior. We cannot simply switch to basing all our actions on purely environmental values. Every day 6 billion people wake up with real needs for food, energy and materials. The challenge for sustainability is to provide for those needs in ways that reduce negative impact on the environment. But any changes made must also be socially acceptable and technically and economically feasible. It is not always easy to balance environmental, social, and economic priorities. Compromise and co-operation with the involvement of government, industry, academia and the environmental movement is required to achieve sustainability. . . .

Coming from British Columbia, born into a third generation forest industry family, and educated in forestry and ecology, it made sense that I would focus on the challenge of defining sustainable forestry. After all, forests are by far the most important environment in British Columbia and they are also by far the most important basis of economic wealth for families and communities.

I soon discovered that trees are just large plants that have evolved the ability to grow long wooden stems. They didn't do that so we could cut them up into lumber and grind them into pulp; they actually had only one purpose in mind and that was to get their needles or leaves higher up above the other plants where the tree could then monopolize the Sun's energy for photosynthesis. When foresters create openings or clearcuts when they harvest trees, one of the reasons for doing it is so the new trees growing back can be in full sunlight. Trees are basically plants that want to be in the sun. If trees wanted to be in the shade they would have been shrubs instead, they would not have spent so much time and energy growing long wooden stems.

"Taken in the right light, clearcuts can actually look quite pretty."

Forests are home to the majority of living species; not the oceans, nor the grasslands, nor the alpine areas, but ecosystems that are dominated by trees. There is a fairly simple reason for this. The living bodies of the trees themselves create a new environment that would not be there in their absence. Now the canopy above is home to millions of birds and insects where there was once only thin air. And beneath the canopy, in the interior of the forest, the environment is now protected from frost and sun and wind. This, in combination with the food provided by the leaves, fruits and even the wood of the trees, creates thousands of new habitats into which new species can evolve, species that could never have existed if it were not for the presence of the living trees.

Logging and Extinction

This gives rise to the obvious concern that if the trees are cut down the habitats or homes will be lost and the species that live in them will die. Indeed, in 1996 the World Wildlife Fund, at a media conference in Geneva, announced that 50,000 species are going extinct each year due to human activity. And the main cause of these 50,000 extinctions, they said, is commercial logging. The story was carried around the world by Associated Press and other media and hundreds of millions of people came to believe that forestry is the main cause of species extinction.

[Since the late 1990s] I have asked the World Wildlife Fund on many occasions to please provide me with a list of some of the species that have supposedly become extinct due to logging. They have not offered up a single example as evidence. In fact, to the best of our scientific knowledge, no species has become extinct in North America due to forestry. . . .

> *"Wood is without a doubt the most renewable material used to build and maintain our civilization."*

It's not as if humans have never caused the extinction of species; they have and the list is quite long. There are three main ways by which humans cause species extinction. First, and perhaps most effective, is simply killing them all, with spears, clubs, and rifles. The passenger pigeon, the dodo bird, the Carolinian parakeet, and back in time, the mammoths and mastodons, are all examples of species that were simply wiped out either for food or because they were pests.

Secondly, the vast clearance of native forests for agriculture. There may have been an orchid in that valley bottom that was found nowhere else. If all the forest is cleared away, burned, plowed, and planted with corn the orchid may disappear forever.

Third, and actually the major cause of species extinction by humans during the past 200 years is the introduction of exotic predators and diseases. In particular, when Europeans colonized Australia, New Zealand, and the other Pacific Islands, including Hawaii, they brought with them rats, cats, foxes, pigs, sheep, goats, chickens and cows, and all the other domestic animals and plants, including their diseases. This resulted in the extinction of hundreds of ground dwelling marsupials and flightless birds, as well as many other species.

We have long lists of species that have become extinct due to these three types of human activity but we do not know of a single species that has become extinct due to forestry. . . .

The Benefits of Clearcutting

We have all been taught since we were children that you should not judge a book by its cover, in other words that beauty is only skin deep. Yet we are still easily tricked into thinking that if we like what we see with our eyes, it must be good, and if we don't like what we see with our eyes, it must be bad. We tend to link our visual impression of what is beautiful and what is ugly with our moral judgment of what is right and wrong. The Sierra Club says, "You don't need a professional forester to tell if a forest is mismanaged—if a forest appears to be mismanaged, it is mismanaged." They want you to believe that the ugly appearance of a recently harvested forest is synonymous with permanent destruction of the environment. And yet, the unsightly sea of stumps is not nuclear waste or a toxic discharge, it is 100 percent organic, and will soon grow back to a beautiful new forest again. All the same, the fact that recently harvested areas of forest appear ugly to our eyes makes for very effective images in the hands of anti-forestry activists.

Taken in the right light, clearcuts can actually look quite pretty. Think, for just a moment, of the clearcut as a temporary meadow. It is temporary because it will not stay that way; it will grow back into a new forest again. But it is meadow-like for the time being because the trees have been removed and now the sun can reach directly to the ground, fostering the growth of plants that could never grow in the shade of the trees. We never think of meadows and clearcuts in the same breath. After all, meadows are lovely places which you can walk across easily in the open sun, find a dry smooth place, lay your picnic blanket down and have a lovely afternoon. Clearcuts, on the other hand, are ugly places full of twisted, broken wood and stumps, and there is no nice smooth, dry place to put down a picnic blanket. These distinctions have nothing to do with biodiversity or science, they are purely matters of human aesthetics. Meadows are actually small deserts where it is too dry for trees to grow. That's why they are so smooth. Meadows are only capable of supporting drought-resistant grasses and herbs. Clearcuts, on the other hand, can support a wider variety of grasses and herbs, as well as woody shrubs and trees. Within a year or two of harvesting, clearcuts will generally have far higher biodiversity than meadows. And within a decade or so they begin to look just as good too.

In the space of a few short years, a clearcut that is very ugly to look at can be transformed into a beautiful sea of blossoms growing from seeds that blow in on the wind after fire. Was the clearcut bad when it looked ugly? Is it good now that it looks beautiful? The fact is, it is a serious mistake to judge the environmental health of the land simply by looking at it from an aesthetic perspective. . . .

Deforestation is a difficult subject for the forest industry because it certainly looks deforested when all the trees are cut down in a given area. Unfortunately for the public's understanding of this term, cutting the trees down is not sufficient in itself to cause deforestation. What really matters is whether the forest is removed permanently, or reforested with new trees. But the unsightly nature of a recently harvested forest, even if it is going to grow back eventually, can easily give the impression of environmental destruction and deforestation. . . .

Use More Wood

You would think that since forestry is the most sustainable of all the primary industries, and that wood is without a doubt the most renewable material used to build and maintain our civilization, that this would give wood a lot of green eco-points in the environmental movement's ledger. Unfortunately, this doesn't seem to be the case. Greenpeace has gone before the United Nations Inter-Governmental Panel on Forests, calling on countries to reduce the amount of wood they use and to adopt "environmentally appropriate substitutes" instead. No list of substitutes is provided. The Sierra Club is calling for "zero cut" and an end to all commercial forestry on federal public lands in the United States. The Rainforest Action Network wants a 75 percent reduction in wood use in North America by the year 2015. I think it is fair to summarize this approach as "cut fewer trees, use less wood." It is my firm belief, as a lifelong environmentalist and ecologist, that this is an anti-environmental policy. Putting aside, for a moment, the importance of forestry for our economy and communities; on purely environmental grounds the policy of "use less wood" is anti-environmental. In particular, it is logically inconsistent with, and diametrically opposed to, policies that would bring about positive results for both climate change and biodiversity conservation. I will explain my reasoning for this belief:

First, it is important to recognize that we do use a tremendous amount of wood. On a daily basis, on average, each of the 6 billion people on Earth uses 3.5 pounds or 1.6 kilos of wood every day, for a total of 3.5 billion tons per year. So why don't we just cut that in half and save vast areas of forest from harvesting? In order to demonstrate the superficial nature of this apparent logic it is necessary to look at what we are doing with all this wood.

> *"So long as people think it is inherently wrong to cut down trees we will continue to behave in a logically inconsistent and dysfunctional manner."*

It comes as a surprise to many people that over half the wood used every year is not for building things but for burning as energy. 60 percent of all wood use is for energy, mainly for cooking and heating in the tropical developing countries where 2.5 billion people depend on wood as their primary source of energy. They cannot afford substitutes because most of them make less than $1000 per year. But even if they could afford substitute fuels they would nearly always have to turn to coal, oil, or natural gas; in other words non-renewable fossil fuels. How are we going to stabilize carbon dioxide emissions from excessive use of fossil fuels . . . if 2.5 billion people switch from a renewable wood energy to non-renewable fossil fuels? Even in cases where fuelwood supplies are not sustainable at present levels of consumption the answer is not to use less wood and switch to non-renewables. The answer is to grow more trees.

25 percent of the wood used in the world is for building

things such as houses and furniture. Every available substitute is non-renewable and requires a great deal more energy consumption to produce. That is because wood is produced in a factory called the forest by renewable solar energy. Wood is essentially the material embodiment of solar energy. Non-renewable building materials such as steel, cement, and plastic must be produced in real factories such as steel mills, cement works, and oil refineries. This usually requires large inputs of fossil fuels inevitably resulting in high carbon dioxide emissions. So, for 70 percent of the wood used each year for energy and building, switching to substitutes nearly always results in increased carbon dioxide emissions, contrary to climate change policy.

15 percent of the wood harvested is used to manufacture pulp and paper mainly for printing, packaging, and sanitary purposes. Fully half of this wood is derived from the wastes from the sawmills which produce the solid wood products for building. Most of the remaining supply is from tree plantations, many of which are established on land that was previously cleared for agriculture. So even if we did stop using wood to make pulp and paper it would not have the effect of "saving" many forests. . . .

It is therefore clear to me that the policy of "use less wood" is anti-environmental because it would result in increased carbon dioxide emissions and a reduction in forested land. I believe the correct policy is a positive rather than a negative one. From an environmental perspective the correct policy is "grow more trees, and use more wood." This can be accomplished in a number of ways.

Managing the Forests Better

First, it is important to place some of the world's forest into permanently protected parks and wilderness reserves where no industrial development occurs. The World Wildlife Fund recommends that 10 percent of the world's forests should be set aside for this purpose. Perhaps it should even be 15 percent. But then the question becomes, how should we manage the remaining 85 to 90 percent of the forest? I believe we should manage it more intensively for higher timber production, keeping in mind the needs of other species in the landscape. By just managing our existing forests better we could dramatically increase the world's supply of wood. In addition, we should expand the geographic extent of our forests, largely by reforesting areas of land that were previously cleared for agriculture. In particular, huge areas of forest have been cleared for domestic animal production to supply us with meat. A modest reduction in meat consumption would open up large areas of land for reforestation. This would be good for our health as well as the health of the environment. . . .

But the general public and our political leaders have been confused by the misguided approach towards forestry taken by much of the environmental movement. So long as people think it is inherently wrong to cut down trees we will continue to behave in a logically inconsistent and dysfunctional manner.

I believe that trees are the answer to many questions about our future on this earth. These include—how can we advance to a more sustainable economy based on renewable fuels and materials? How can we improve literacy and sanitation in developing countries while reversing deforestation and protecting wildlife at the same time? How can we reduce the amount of greenhouse gases emitted to the atmosphere, carbon dioxide in particular? How can we increase the amount of land that will support a greater diversity of species? How can we help prevent soil erosion and provide clean air and water? How can we make this world more beautiful and green? The answer is, by growing more trees and using more wood both as a substitute for non-renewable fossil fuels and materials such as steel, concrete, and plastic, and as paper products for printing, packaging, and sanitation.

4

The Paper Industry Is Destroying Forests and Native Species

Alex Shoumatoff

A former staff writer at the New Yorker *and contributing editor at* Vanity Fair, *Alex Shoumatoff is the author of ten books, including* Legends of the American Desert.

Thirteen southern states produce nearly 60 percent of the wood used in the United States. The heart of this wood-producing region is the Cumberland Plateau in Tennessee. Unlike most western forests that are managed by the U.S. Forest Service, the woodlands of Tennessee are mostly on private property owned by multinational paper products corporations. Largely free from government regulations, these corporations are using huge machines to mow down native oaks, hickories, and sycamores that are then ground into pulp to make newspaper, toilet paper, shopping bags, and other paper products. The barren land is replanted with a single tree species, the loblolly pine, which has been genetically engineered to grow two to five times faster than native trees. The paper industry supports the Sustainable Forestry Initiative (SFI), whose goals are supposedly to protect wildlife habitat, biodiversity, and soil. However, in reality the SFI is a fraud that permits businesses to abuse the environment while hiding behind this supposedly "green" initiative.

If there were an international tribunal that prosecuted crimes against the planet, like the one in The Hague that deals with crimes against humanity, what is happening on the Cumberland Plateau in eastern Tennessee would undoubtedly be indictable.

The crime—one of many clandestine ecocides American corporations are committing around the world—has taken place over three decades. About 200,000 acres on this tableland have already been clearcut by the paper industry, and the cutting continues. Where once grew some of the most biologically rich hardwood forest in North America's Temperate Zone (which extends from the Gulf of Mexico to southern Canada), there are now row after row of fast-growing loblolly pine trees genetically engineered to yield the most pulp in the shortest time. But the paper industry's insatiable appetite for timber has met with unexpected competition from an equally voracious insect. In the last four years, an estimated 50 to 70 percent of the pines planted on the plateau have been devoured by the southern pine beetle. The entire South has been ravaged by the worst outbreak in its history of this native predator of pine trees, caused by the tremendous increase in the amount of pine available for it to eat on the industry plantations that have replaced the native forest. Unable to salvage its dead timber, the paper industry has been losing hundreds of millions of dollars. Yet it seems still committed to destroying what remains of the extraordinarily lush forest on the Cumberland Plateau, which, along with eastern Tennessee's Great Valley and the Cumberland Mountains, has the highest concentration of endangered species in North America. The loss of biodiversity is tragic but also absurd economically; it doesn't even make good business sense.

"The loss of biodiversity is tragic but also absurd economically; it doesn't even make good business sense."

Not many people are aware of what is taking place. Nearly 90 percent of the Cumberland Plateau is in private hands and exempt from all but a few government regulations. The federal and state agencies that are supposed to be regulating the paper, timber, and mining industries are populated with these companies' former executives and have come to view these industries as clients whose permits and projects should be facilitated rather than scrutinized. The cozy relationship that exists between Tennessee's public and private sectors, and the impunity and magnitude of the environmental destruction taking place on the plateau, are what you might expect in Guatemala or deep in the Brazilian Amazon, not in our republic, where there are supposed to be laws that protect our wilderness treasures and prosecute conflicts of interest. But a quarter of the world's paper and 60 percent of America's wood products are being produced in the South, and the will to address the abuses of the paper industry, which contributes millions of dollars to the campaign coffers of politicians around the country, just isn't there—certainly not in Tennessee.

"A quarter of the world's paper and 60 percent of America's wood products are being produced in the South, and the will to address the abuses. . . just isn't there."

There's another reason for the lack of public awareness: Much of the devastation is hidden from view by thin "beauty strips" of native forest left along the plateau's highways. The only way to get the full picture is to go up in a small plane and see it from the air.

A Flying Classroom

So early this past September [2003] I took off from Knoxville in a Cessna 182 piloted by Hume Davenport, the founder of a nonprofit, conservation-minded aviation service called SouthWings. Hume, whose ancestors came to the Cumberlands in 1801, has provided his "flying classroom" to dozens of journalists, environmentalists, and policymakers trying to grasp the enormity of what is happening on the plateau.

The Cumberlands are made up of the Cumberland Plateau and the mountains and foothills on its edges. The plateau itself is a 400-mile-long tableland that is the tail end of the Appalachian Plateau; it extends from West Virginia and Virginia down into Kentucky and Tennessee on a southwesterly diagonal and peters out in Alabama. The part in Tennessee tapers from 55 miles wide to about 38 and covers 6,875 square miles—an area larger than the state of Connecticut. About 85 percent of it is still covered with the native woodland. Some of the last remaining large stands of the Appalachian mixed mesophytic forest (where a variety of hardwoods grow in moderately moist conditions) are here, but the plateau was "pretty much raked over the coals a century ago," Hume explained, and most of the trees are second growth. . . .

> *"Because [the soil is] thin and sandy, they have to spray massive amounts of fertilizer from crop dusters so the pine trees can grow. It's complete insanity."*

Soon we were over the Cumberland Mountains, whose peaks range from 2,000 to 4,000 feet. . . .

In nearby Pioneer, we made a few passes over the Royal Blue chip mill, owned by International Paper, the biggest paper company in the world. A chip mill is a satellite facility, where hardwoods of smaller diameter and plantation pines are diced into wafers that are taken to a mother mill, to be dissolved into pulp. The larger hardwoods are sawed into boards at another mill.

There are 156 chip mills and 103 pulp mills in the 13 southern states. More than a hundred of the chip mills were constructed between 1987 and 1997, when chip exports (mostly to Japan) escalated by 500 percent. Eleven mills get their wood from the plateau. Royal Blue alone eats up 7,000 acres of hardwood trees a year—oaks, tulip poplars, and half a dozen other species—from within a 75-mile radius. We could see two miniature logging trucks coming down the highway far below us, another being unloaded, and four waiting behind it. A huge claw suspended from a crane picked up the logs and fed them into the chipper, which spewed the chips out a pipe directly onto railroad cars that would take them to the Blue Ridge Paper Company's Pigeon River mill in Canton, North Carolina. Most of the wood here is "gatewood": Few, if any, questions are asked about where the timber comes from or the manner in which it was harvested.

We banked southwest and, heading right down the middle of the plateau, began to see massive devastation. "This isn't

Ma-and-Pa, let's-clear-40-acres stuff," Hume yelled through the headphones. "It's big, industrial tree farming. When they took out the big trees a century ago, at least they left the little ones to take their place. But now they're scraping off the soil, right down to the bedrock. Because it's thin and sandy, they have to spray massive amounts of fertilizer from crop dusters so the pine trees can grow. It's complete insanity. Most of the trees they're planting are being chewed up by beetles. Look at these plantations. It's a graveyard."

Beetles Having a Field Day

Below us, vast stands of dead gray loblolly pine, covering hundreds of acres, had been skeletonized by the southern pine beetle, Dendroctonus frontalis. The beetle breaks out every 10 to 30 years—what triggers the outbreak is not understood—and attacks native longleaf, shortleaf, Virginia, black, yellow, Table Mountain, and white pines that are sparsely scattered in the hardwood forest. But with many tens of thousands of acres of monoculture pine on the plateau, the beetles have been having a field day. The beetles are even chewing up saplings and the prize conifers in people's yards. In a race against the plague, the paper companies are forced to harvest their timber before it is mature, creating a glut of scrawny "bugwood" on the market. This has severely depressed the price of pulp. Couple this with the hundreds of millions of dollars of lost revenue from the timber the beetles have beaten them to, and competition from Canada's timber, and it's clear why the South's paper companies are in trouble.

The biggest landowner on the southern plateau is Bowater, the biggest manufacturer of newsprint in the country and one of the largest producers of the free-sheet coated paper used for glossy magazines and catalogs. Now, as we flew south over Crossville, the commercial hub of the southern plateau and a burgeoning retirement community, houses abruptly gave way to Bowater's industrial tree farms and huge squares of mangled wasteland that had been hacked out of the forest and not yet replanted. "This plateau has been ransacked," Hume said sadly. He took us over a particularly vast mutilated swath that some activists have dubbed the Triangle of Destruction, but it is only one of many.

The only clearcutting I had seen on this scale was in the Amazon 25 years ago. Every merchantable stick below us had been taken, streambeds and banks had been torn up and gouged by recklessly driven machines, and the understory shrubs and stripped-off branches and other debris had been bulldozed into windrows, some of which had been torched and were shooting up sooty flames. "It used to be just Bowater," Hume said, "but in the last few years International Paper and J.M. Huber—a wood products company—have gotten into the act. When Huber showed up in '97, we saw a vast increase, maybe a doubling, of the clearcutting." Four million additional acres of the South's forests are being converted to pine plantations each year, according to the U.S. Forest Service, and the conversion rate is expected to double by 2040.

On the plateau, this translates to an annual holocaust of about 3 million trees, 14 million if you count smaller trees and pines. What's driving this? Consider that a quarter of the world's paper is produced in the South. The average American consumes about half a ton a year—that's factoring in toddlers and oldsters and people on life support. This is 111 times the per capita consumption in India, 300 times that of some African countries. Much of this consists of glossy catalogs and other junk mail, which I get a two-foot stack of each week; the sections of the paper that I chuck without even glancing at them (the *Washington Post* and other newspapers are printed on Bowater paper taken straight from the plateau); the inch-high stack of napkins we're handed whenever we get takeout; the 10 feet of toilet paper we rip off to clean ourselves. As one environmentalist put it arrestingly: "We're wiping our asses with habitat."

Endangered Species

The Appalachian mixed mesophytic forest, which still covers five-sixths of the Cumberland Plateau, evolved without disturbance for hundreds of millions of years, because the glaciers never got this far south. Genetically distinct populations of plants, salamanders, and other organisms arose in the hollows, coves, and gulfs that pleat the plateau. There are nine endemic species of lungless plethodon salamander here. But amphibians are among the first victims of deforestation and of the desiccation and silting up of streams that ensue. The plateau also boasts 20 mussel and 40 crayfish species that evolved here and are found nowhere else. Even more diverse are the 231 fish species, of which 67 are endemic: 16 minnows, five suckers, two cave springfish, one killifish, one pygmy sunfish, one sculpin, and an incredible 41 darters. New species are being discovered all the time; others will probably be wiped out before they are identified.

The Cumberland Plateau is believed to have the highest concentration of caves and of cave-dwelling invertebrate species in North America. Three species of bat are endangered or threatened, and 12 of rodent. The plateau is also a major nexus for migratory birds, a pit stop for many species as they wind their way back and forth from South America or the Caribbean to the Canadian boreal forest, as well as the home of many year-round inhabitants.

> *"Four million additional acres of the South's forests are being converted to pine plantations each year . . . and the conversion rate is expected to double by 2040."*

The original forest still stands in only a few places on the plateau. Starting in the 1870s, as the Northeast was industrializing and its cities were mushrooming, there was a great demand for wood. The agents of coal and timber corporations came down and hornswoggled the unschooled people of the Cumberlands out of their trees, paying 40 cents (in the coin of the day) for a 175 foot-tall tulip poplar, offering a new squirrel gun for 3,000 acres of timber rights. Pretty much every decent-sized tree, except the ones in the most inaccessible coves and hollows, was sawed down and floated down the Cumberland or Sequatchie rivers or, beginning in the 1890s, taken out by rail. The logging boom ended in 1901. Then they went after the coal, and in the seventies, when most of that was gone, they started in on the trees again. . . .

The Debate over Sustainable Forestry

Climbing back into the Cessna, we rose above the University of the South's Gothic spires and flew southeast, off the plateau and into the Great Valley. Before long an enormous industrial complex—Bowater's Calhoun Mill—hove into view. The largest manufacturer of newsprint in the United States, it has been operating since 1954 and sits on the Hiwassee River, a tributary of the Tennessee. As we circled it from several thousand feet above, the rotten-egg fumes of methyl mercaptan and hydrogen sulfide emitted by its digesters penetrated the cabin of the Cessna and gave us all nausea. This is a pervasive smell in much of the rural South. Bowater alone has 12 pulp and paper mills in the U.S., Canada, and South Korea, supported by 1.4 million acres of owned or leased timberland in the U.S., a large portion of which—about 700,000—is in the Southeast. It also owns 32 million acres of timber-cutting rights in Canada. Besides manufacturing 18 percent of North America's newsprint and 7 percent of the world's, Bowater produces five kinds of "market pulp" one of which—Calhoun southern bleached hardwood kraft pulp—is made here, from "premium grade southern mixed hardwoods," as the company's website explains. The hardwoods come from the Cumberland Plateau, where Bowater owns about 160,000 acres. We could see a continuous procession of logging trucks entering and exiting the compound, adding their loads to a pile of logs covering an area the size of several football fields and three stories high. "The scale of this operation is just intimidating," Hume said. "It's hard to fathom how many trees, how many acres of forest, it must take to feed it." . . .

> *"The SFI . . . allows enormous habitat destruction. It's a fig leaf that tolerates all kinds of bad practices, business as usual."*

[A few days later] I put in a call to Barry Graden, Bowater's southeastern woodlands operations manager. . . .

Barry and I [had] a long talk on the phone, during which he described all the good things Bowater was supposedly doing on the plateau. But it bore little resemblance to what I had seen from the air and from the ground. Barry explained that Bowater subscribed to something called the Sustainable Forestry Initiative (SFI), whose objectives included "protecting wildlife habitat, biodiversity, and watersheds, conserving soil," and attending to the "visual impact" and "the aesthetics" of timber operations. Barry himself was in charge of Bowater's compliance with the initiative for the Southeast. More than 100 million acres of American forestland are enrolled in the program. But not everyone shares Barry's enthusiasm for the initiative. Activists contend that it competes with—and intentionally obscures—another protocol known as the Forest Stewardship Council (FSC), which was developed in 1993 by environmental and other activist groups and businesses. A number of large corporations, including Home Depot and Ikea, now participate in the Forest Stewardship Council by agreeing to purchase wood, whenever available, that is FSC-certified—that is, harvested in accordance with sustainable logging and plantation practices.

"The paper industry's response was to confuse the issue," [environmental activist] Allen Hershkowitz explained, "and counter the market momentum generated by the Forest Stewardship Council. International Paper will stamp on its paper that it is complying with the SFI, and people will think it's the FSC. It's a classic weakening technique. But the SFI sucks; it allows enormous habitat destruction. It's a fig leaf that tolerates all kinds of bad practices, business as usual. Everything that is happening on the plateau is SFI-certified."

Barry assured me, "Everything we do is verified by an environmental auditor. We provide our customers, the media, and environmental organizations the opportunity to see for themselves that we're doing what we say we do." Apparently that didn't include me.

Barry also claimed that Bowater made every effort to protect endangered species, but Lee Barclay, the supervisor of the U.S. Fish and Wildlife Service's field office in charge of protecting the federally listed endangered and threatened species in Tennessee, complained that he often can't get on the paper companies' land to see what is there.

"They have to give us permission to enter," Barclay told me. "It's private land, so we have no authority unless we have proof that they are knowingly thumbing their noses at the Endangered Species Act, and you need dead bodies to do that. Their attitude is, if we let them get a foot in the door, we'll never be able to close it."

Just this October [2003], the discovery of a new species of salamander on the plateau was announced. Who knows what other undiscovered flora and fauna are on the 90 percent of it that is in private hands? . . .

Changing Business Practices

In 1996, Cielo [Sand] and Danna Smith, who had worked on forest-protection campaigns for Greenpeace, founded the Dogwood Alliance, an umbrella group of 72 grassroots religious, student, and community activist organizations concerned with protecting the forests of the South. Last year [2003] Dogwood and its partners got Staples, the $11 billion office supply company and one of International Paper's biggest customers, to commit to phasing out products from endangered forests and to use an average of 30 percent postconsumer recycled fiber for all its paper products, which was an enormous victory. Dogwood considers "market strategy"—leveraging the paper companies through their consumers—as the best way to stop what they are doing on the plateau. "Hitting them where it hurts is the only language they understand" Allen Hershkowitz agreed. "Some of Staples' paper probably comes from the Royal Blue mill, and they need to know this. A lot more chain-of-custody work—tracing the fiber from the forest to the mill to the consumers—has to be done. Office Depot is another big customer of International Paper, and it also buys from the Weyerhaeuser paper company's mill in Kingsport, Tennessee, which is just off the plateau and probably sources from it. Office Depot has to be pressured into making the same commitment that Staples and Home Depot have. Then we can get the three of them competing to have the greenest paper on the block. But first, a lot more dots have to be connected."

As for Bowater, because some of its mills supply newsprint or market pulp to practically every major publication in the country—the *New York Times*, the *Boston Globe*, the Knight-Ridder and Gannett chains; *The New Yorker*, *Vanity Fair*, *Vogue*, *GQ*, *Conde Nast Traveler* (which gives an annual environmental award), and the rest of the Conde Nast empire; *Golf Digest*, *TV Guide*, even the *Utne Reader*—the leveraging potential is very promising. With the Dogwood Alliance as its main local partner, Allen is organizing an NRDC [National Resources Defense Council] campaign that will invest five to seven million dollars into saving the Cumberland Plateau over the next 10 years. . . .

So things are starting to move. The Nature Conservancy and World Wildlife Fund have initiatives of their own to save the plateau. . . . The Cumberland Plateau is poised at a critical moment in its history. If the opportunity is squandered, if people simply keep playing the "Tennessee Waltz," they will awaken one day to an irreversible tragedy, just as the song says: Now I know just how much I have lost.

5

Environmental Lawsuits Are Destroying Forest Communities

Valerie Richardson

Valerie Richardson is a journalist for Insight on the News *and its sister publication, the* Washington Times.

Almost every time the Forest Service decides to harvest timber in a national forest, environmental groups file lawsuits to stop the logging. When these projects are stopped, it causes severe economic hardship for nearby communities that depend on logging. While lawsuits take years to wind through the courts, sawmills close, unemployment grows, and schools are forced to make drastic budget cuts. Managing forest lands through lawsuits and appeals leaves forest communities vulnerable as people struggle to survive.

Look in any direction along this stretch of rural Idaho near Cascade. It's all trees—thousands upon thousands of acres of lodge-pole pine and Douglas fir, cascading down hills and blanketing mountains as far as the eye can see. For a century, the trees of the Boise, Payette, Nez Perce and Clearwater national forests provided the people here with shelter, work, recreation and a way of life.

No longer. As poet Samuel Coleridge once observed about the ocean—"Water, water everywhere, / Nor any drop to drink" —so Idaho's forests are filled with millions of trees that cannot

Valerie Richardson, "In Idaho, the Loggers Are Losing: Idahoans Have Watched Their Lumber Industry Grind to a Halt as Environmentalists Use the Courts to Stop Logging in National Forests," *Insight on the News*, vol. 17, December 24, 2001, p. 28.

be touched. For the last decade, timber communities throughout the Pacific Northwest have waged a legal and public-relations battle with environmental groups; by all accounts and on every front, the loggers are losing.

President Theodore Roosevelt's vision of maintaining the national forests as the nation's lumber supply was replaced during the Clinton administration by the idea that forests should be preserved in their natural state. The amount of timber that could be harvested was reduced drastically, both by the administration's moratorium on road-building and by the legal system, as environmentalists took to the courts to stop the logging.

That shift has come at a price. There are more trees and more old growth, but also more disease and dead wood. There are fewer chain saws in the forests, but also fewer mills, homes and families. And within the small, wooded hamlets whose denizens have cut and replanted the trees for generations, there is poverty, dislocation, anger and a sense of disbelief that slowly is turning into resignation.

"Within the small, wooded hamlets whose denizens have cut and replanted the trees for generations, there is poverty, dislocation, anger and a sense of disbelief."

"It's tough, especially for the kids, because they look around and there are trees everywhere you look," says Dick Vandenburg, a Cascade City Council member. "They don't understand the politics."

Idaho and the rest of the Pacific Northwest have watched the timber economy plummet during the last decade, taking with it a dozen mills and at least 30,000 jobs. The reasons include automation and greater efficiency, falling lumber prices and stiff competition from cheaper Canadian lumber.

"The reason the mills closed is soft prices, imports from Canada and the timber industry's willingness to move to other countries because of relaxed environmental standards under NAFTA [North American Free Trade Agreement]," says Roger Singer, director of the Sierra Club's Idaho chapter. "The sudden downturn in the industry is due to market forces, not environmental challenges."

People in the timber industry maintain they could have handled such fluctuations without closing the mills. What they couldn't handle was the political assault from the environmental movement.

"All these mills have been around for almost a century," says Steve Bliss, a former mill worker and union representative from Horseshoe Bend. "They've been through economic upturns and downturns. They went through the Depression. But you can't operate without raw materials. It has nothing to do with the economy and nothing to do with demand. It has everything to do with the environmental movement and political correctness."

Lawsuits and Timber Sales

Each year, the U.S. Forest Service offers stands of timber for sale as determined under the forest plan, then takes bids and awards the sale to the highest bidder. (The national forests are distinct from wilderness areas, where trees by law cannot be harvested; in Idaho, where 68 percent of the Gem State's 53 million acres is run by the federal government, 7.5 percent of the land is classified as wilderness.) Starting in the mid-1980s, however, environmental groups began stepping up their opposition to timber sales in the national forests. Recently, they've managed to bring the process to a grinding halt by filing legal challenges, or appeals, to most timber sales.

The appeals usually are based on perceived problems with the sale, such as a failure to take into account endangered species or sensitive wildlife habitat. Sometimes they are successful, and a judge halts the sale. "The reason we're successful is because the Forest Service isn't playing by the rules," says John McCarthy, wildlife director of the Idaho Conservation League, which is responsible for many of the challenges. "They can't account for old growth and how it affects endangered species. We can always find experts on the inside who will say, 'They're doing it wrong.'"

Even when the appeals fail, the process can drag on for years. That's too much time for small logging outfits and mills, which can go out of business waiting for a challenge to move through the legal system.

"You have one year to harvest whitewood [softwood deciduous trees]" says Cascade Mayor Larry Walters. "But as soon as you put a sale up, you get hit with appeals. By the time it's resolved, that wood is no good anymore. It's just such a waste."

In February [2001], Boise Cascade Corp. announced that it would shut down its mills in Cascade and Emmett, laying off 400 workers. While some critics blamed poor management, Chairman George J. Harad cited lack of raw materials. The closures came as the end of an era for Boise Cascade, which has seen its mills in Idaho decline from five to none. "Despite an adequate supply of timber, under the policies of the Clinton administration and pressure from environmental groups, the amount of timber offered for commercial harvest has declined more than 90 percent over the past five years," says Harad.

The ripple effect led to the closure of half-a-dozen related businesses in Cascade, ranging from a rental-equipment outlet to a flower shop. Soon the modest one-story homes in Cascade's neighborhoods were peppered with "For Sale" signs as families sought jobs elsewhere in the Northwest. After the mill closed, as many as 70 families moved, including some whose roots in the town of about 1,000 went back three generations. "I don't know what's worse, to leave town or to stay here and watch everyone else leave," says Vandenburg.

Those fortunate enough to find jobs in Cascade were forced to take substantial pay cuts. Jobs at the Boise Cascade mill paid between $12 and $19 an hour with "the best benefits package in Idaho," says Ron Lundquist, a former mill worker. He now helps manage a trailer park, a job that pays well at $16 an hour but provides bare-bones benefits, not to mention less satisfaction. "I enjoy this job," Lundquist says. "But I was raised in a resource family. There's something to be said for making something from a natural resource. It's rewarding because you're building something."

Trying to Diversify

Faced with double-digit unemployment and no second coming of the timber industry in sight, Idaho logging towns are trying to diversify their economies by luring other businesses, starting with tourism. When Cascade's mill closed, the town received a series of state grants, including one from the Idaho Tourism Council, to raise the town's profile. Given the beauty of the forests, rivers and lakes, spotlighting rafting, boating and hiking opportunities came as a natural move. "The governor [Republican Dirk Kempthorne] has been tremendous," Vandenburg says. "We've received grant after grant."

Tourism offers its own set of problems, however. The work is seasonal—strong in the summer but virtually nonexistent in the winter—and the jobs don't pay as well as millwork. In Riggins, just north of Cascade, the town has a thriving river-rafting business, but the investment hasn't paid off as well as locals had hoped.

"They're relying on tourism for their funds and, frankly, there isn't any money in that," says Wayne Davis, superintendent of the local school district. "You get a few backpackers, a few rafters, but there's nothing to sustain jobs."

Tourism also tends to change the complexion of towns. Locals point to the example of McCall, about 30 miles north of Cascade, where the town managed to replace a closed mill with tourism, then watched as wealthy retirees moved in, drove up housing prices and began pushing out the middle class. "McCall has gone from a working-man's community to a richman's playground," says Dave Rosen, a former coworker of Lundquist.

Greater Fire Danger

A recent rash of forest fires, which locals blame on the Forest Service's official reluctance to clear dead and diseased wood, has been another impediment. Here again residents have met opposition from environmentalists, who argue that fire clears the deadwood more naturally than chain saws. "I'd rather see us use fire as the tool of first choice than chain saws as the tool of first choice," says McCarthy of the Idaho Conservation League.

> *"They're relying on tourism for their funds and, frankly, there isn't any money in that."*

Green groups also have fought efforts to clear the accumulating "fuel" through Forest Service salvage sales, which allow loggers to clear dead trees and brush. "The thing about salvage is that it doesn't just look at dead trees—it also looks at what's going to die," McCarthy says, adding that his group recently stopped a large salvage sale in North Idaho. "And you can't predict what's going to die and what's not."

Phil Davis, a Valley County commissioner and rancher, argues that the recent fires have been anything but natural, burning so hot and so long that the land takes decades to regenerate. He noted that 25 percent of the Payette National Forest has burned in the last few years, while the summer of 2000 fires left blackened an area the size of Rhode Island (1,052 square miles).

"The reason we're in this situation is that these people, in the name of the environment, have made it so the Forest Service cannot manage their lands," Davis says. "And it's been to the detriment of the environment."

Hurting Public Schools

Perhaps the biggest untold story from the timber economy's decline is its impact on public schools. Most schools rely on property taxes for the bulk of their funding. In the West, however, where most of the land is federally owned, there isn't a big enough tax base to maintain rural schools. As a result, the Forest Service sends 25 percent of its sale receipts back to the state. Of that, 70 percent goes toward state road projects and 30 percent goes to schools.

Consequently, as timber profits have fallen, so has money for education. Cascade has just begun to feel the pinch, but in communities whose mills shut down five or six years ago, school officials have been forced to fire teachers, eliminate elective classes, cut sports and music, and even trim the school week down from five days to four.

In Grangeville, where the Ida-Pine Mills closed [in 1996], the district has lost 400 students in four years and seen its annual timber payments fall from $1.3 million to $225,000. The biggest hit came two years ago, when the district was forced to cut its budget by $600,000.

"In order to make the budget balance, we had to cut all our sports, our extracurricular activities, drama, debate and our food service," Superintendent Wayne Davis recalls. "It was devastating to anyone involved in extracurricular activities, just devastating.". . .

With 300 employees, the school district is now the largest employer in Grangeville. The town of 7,226 has had some success in attracting new businesses, but has yet to lure any company that can approach the mill's payroll. Still, families are reluctant to leave. Davis attributes their loyalty to the community's values.

"My guess is if you go into this parking lot, half of the cars would have the keys in them," he says. "A lady once said to me,

'If somebody was stranded and needed a vehicle, you would want them to use it.' The value system here is pretty strong. But we've got the second-highest unemployment in the state, so I worry about that.". . .

Not long ago, many communities held out hope that the mills would come back. Locals note that demand for paper products and lumber hasn't abated, and that Canadian loggers, aided by a pro-timber government, are growing rich off the U.S. lumber market. They also are encouraged by the Bush administration. Shortly after taking office, President George W. Bush put the brakes on the Clinton administration's plan to rope off 40 million acres of forest as roadless areas, a move that would have cut off access to yet more timber. On Oct. 31 [2001], the Commerce Department agreed to impose tariffs of as much as 40 percent on Canadian lumber, citing trade practices that have given the Canadians an unfair advantage.

"I think [Bush officials] want this to change, but they're politicians, too," says [Gary] Stears, the high-school principal. "Even though they're friendlier to natural resources, they're subject to the same pushes and pulls. But I'm much more optimistic than before."

Others say it's time to move on. "People are resigned to it," Davis says. "They're making alternative plans. We don't want to live on the false illusion that it's all going to be okay tomorrow."

Kempthorne predicts a future in which most logging on national forests is tied to forest health. "It probably won't be cutting for the sake of cutting; it'll be for clearing the fuel load on the national forests," he says. "The facts now prove that if we don't reduce the fuel load, we'll continue to see the forests blackened.". . .

"The pendulum is probably going to swing back, but for a lot of these towns it's too late," says Bliss, the former mill worker and union representative. "There's never going to be another sawmill in Horseshoe Bend or Cascade—it would cost $50 million in today's dollars to build it."

For anyone who lives in these woods, however, it doesn't take much to restore their faith in the forest's ability to provide for them. "You drive out five minutes in any direction and you're in forest," Cascade School Principal Bill Leaf says. "My father logged the same lands that my grandfather was logging with a horse and teams. It's been here for generations and it's still beautiful land. It hasn't been pilfered."

6

The Actions of Environmentalists Have Not Led to More Forest Fires

Steve Bonowski

Steve Bonowski is the chair of the Colorado Mountain Club (CMC) Conservation Committee, a member of the CMC board of directors, and a member of the Colorado State Trails Committee.

Many politicians and government officials blame recent forest fires in the West on environmentalists and their lawsuits against logging and forest thinning. In fact, only a small percentage of fuel reduction and brush thinning projects are challenged in court by environmentalists, and fewer still are decided in their favor. Those pointing fingers at environmentalists are using tragedy to disguise the fact that most wildfires are caused by drought, hot weather, and high winds. Reducing the threat of fire in the future will require that all interests work together to seek solutions and that politicians stop the anti-environmentalist rhetoric.

As wildfires rage in Colorado and throughout the West [in the summer of 2002], opportunistic politicians are rushing not to put out the flames but instead fan them. The newest trend on Capitol Hill and in governors' mansions around the West is to bash environmentalists unashamedly by blaming

Steve Bonowski, "Did Enviros Cause Western Wildfires?" *Trail & Timberline OnLine*, www.cmc.org, 2003.

them for the recent western forest fires.

In Arizona, Governor Jane Hull and U.S. Senator Jon Kyl blamed "obstructionist environmentalists from the East Coast" for their [2002] wildfires—due to opposition to logging. From Montana, Governor Judy Martz blamed western wildfires on "environmental terrorism." Martz also stated that actions by environmental groups to halt timber sales and logging may be responsible for forest fires.

> *"Facts . . . clearly illustrate that environmentalist appeals and litigation are not a significant cause of wildfires."*

Colorado is not immune to such rhetoric. U.S. Senator Ben Campbell accused environmentalists of filing frivolous lawsuits that interfere with sound forest management policies that would thin forests. Campbell opined that an estimated forty percent of Forest Service work at the national forest level is done to insulate the service from these lawsuits. Two Colorado congressmen, Representative [Scott] McInnis and [Tom] Tancredo, joined in with their own similar accusations. Even the *Rocky Mountain News* got into the enviro-bashing act. A June 27 [2002] editorial pointed a big finger at seven environmental groups for "fighting the government's very modest management plans for years" in the Pike–San Isabel National Forest.

National Rhetoric

Anti-environmental rhetoric flourishes at the national level as well. Interior Secretary Gale Norton offered that there may be evidence to link environmentalists with delays in wildfire prevention programs. According to Norton, "We certainly see the effects of delay and analysis paralysis."

Mark Rey, Undersecretary for Natural Resources and Environment in the Department of Agriculture, joined the fray. Rey, a former official in the timber industry, asked the Forest Service to provide details on appeals and lawsuits by environmental groups that may have blocked or delayed fire prevention projects. Rey also requested a list of projects rejected by the Service due to potential legal concerns, and information about any extra time and money spent to immunize projects against legal action.

Forest [Service] Chief Dale Bosworth joined in the chorus, stating, "Had we been doing fuels removal from these forests for eight or ten years, fire wouldn't be burning the way it is now." Anti-environmental fringe organizations such as People for the USA are also jumping on the bandwagon, taking advantage of the climate to undermine environmental organizations any way they can.

The finger-pointing from politicians and others has been so shrill that almost any pragmatic citizen would begin to doubt its veracity. A careful review of pertinent points shows almost immediately that the rhetoric directed at environmental groups is not supported by fact. The primary reasons for the wildfires are the heavy fuel loads in the forests and the historic drought, following nearly a century of fire suppression by land managers

Anyone growing up in the mid–twentieth century is familiar with Smokey the Bear and his mantra: "Only You Can Prevent Forest Fires." However, in the past twenty years, ecologists began to realize that fire is a critical and necessary part of forest ecosystem rejuvenative processes.

> *"Environmentalists have consistently supported thinning projects where small diameter trees and brushy undergrowth are removed and large trees are left in place."*

Moreover, the facts also clearly illustrate that environmentalist appeals and litigation are not a significant cause of wildfires. In a study published in August, 2001, the General Accounting Office, the auditing agency of Congress, evaluated some 1,670 fuels reduction projects by the Forest Service. Only twenty were appealed, and not all the appeals were done by environmental organizations. None had been litigated.

In Colorado in the past year, the Forest Service had completed necessary environmental analyses on some 104 fuels reduction projects. A timber project on the Upper Blue River in Summit County was one of the few appealed by environmentalists. The same project was also appealed by the ski industry. It is worth noting that this particular project was planned in high elevation spruce/fir forest where fire risk is low, rather than in the urban/forest interface area [where people build houses], the so-called "red zone."

Another statistic worth considering is that about half of the appeals filed by environmental organizations on timber sales are successful, highlighting the fact that the Forest Service is failing to follow its own regulations and federal law in developing sale proposals.

What of the Hayman Fire [in Colorado], and the finger-pointing there? Chief Bosworth suggested indirectly that if the agency could have started thinning eight to ten years ago, the fire might not have burned so fiercely. Yet, it was only in 1999 that the Service first proposed significant thinning projects for the Pike Forest as part of a larger management program, the Upper South Platte (USP) project. Conservationists did not challenge any part of the proposals to thin in some twenty square miles of forests in roaded areas close to communities and homes. An appeal was filed on a backcountry area far from settled areas proposed for logging. Moreover, this particular segment was also appealed by the timber industry. Finally, ninety-eight percent of the Hayman fire occurred outside of the area impacted by the citizen appeals.

The Science, Politics, and Economics of Thinning

Would Hayman have been less devastating had thinning already been done? This will be assessed post-fire, especially in some areas owned and thinned by the Denver Water Department. But thinning may not have helped much, given the drought and weather conditions at the time of the fire. As an example, on June 8 [2002], firefighters working the Hayman were confronting temperatures in the 90s, single digit humidity, and westerly winds of 35 miles per hour. It is unlikely, given those conditions, that even thinned areas would have slowed a fire.

Even so, the scientific evidence to date regarding the efficacy of thinning is mixed. Anecdotal evidence from Arizona indicates thinning there may have helped slow the [2002] Rodeo-Chediski fire. Conversely, in 2000, the Jasper fire in the Black Hills (South Dakota) National Forest burned 80,000 acres, much of it in areas that had already been commercially thinned. A problem with thinning is that the slash (brush, small trees) has to be removed to lessen the fire risk. Commercial logging operations generally leave large piles of slash that can increase fire danger in logged areas.

Thinning, too, is in the eye of the beholder. Timber interests want to log the more profitable big, fire resistant, trees. Environmentalists have consistently supported thinning projects where small diameter trees and brushy undergrowth are removed and large trees are left in place. They are, however, wary of "stewardship" projects that involve mass logging of large diameter trees in backcountry areas distant from private land and homes.

It is also worth noting that in the past twenty years, almost every approved timber sale in the Intermountain West has lost money. That is, the cost of building access roads and cutting trees is more than the value of the timber. The U.S. taxpayers make up the difference. It would seem that if taxpayers have to pay no matter what, then the logical action is to clear the undergrowth and leave the bigger trees in place.

The Forest Service produced a report in late June, 2002, showing that forty-eight percent of 326 thinning projects nationwide in 2001 and early 2002 were appealed. Six percent were litigated. However, a careful review of this study reveals some . . . "books cooking."

Prescribed burns were removed, and appeals from the timber industry were ignored. Also ignored were thinning projects proposed for the backcountry where fire danger for homes is low to non-existent, instead of being proposed for the "red zone." In Colorado, the bark beetle reduction project on the Routt Forest is included as an appealed project, even though this project has nothing to do with fire risk and is not to be funded with fire money. The GAO [General Accounting Office] has admitted that its report was done quickly. . . .

Much must, and will, be done to lessen the danger from fire to private property in the future and to allow fire to take its natural course in places where communities aren't threatened. The best way to do this work is with every interest sitting down together peacefully, without inappropriate finger-pointing and political rhetoric.

7

The U.S. Forest Service Must Not Suppress All Forest Fires

Forest Service Employees for Environmental Ethics

The Forest Service Employees for Environmental Ethics is made up of thousands of Forest Service employees, government resource managers, and activists working to change the Forest Service's land management philosophy.

The U.S. Forest Service spends billions of dollars putting out forest fires every year. This practice needs to be changed. Forest managers must be allowed to let some fires burn themselves out. Fires are a necessary part of forest ecology and are useful for thinning forests, fertilizing the soil, providing animal habitats, and helping some tree species to flourish. When fires are continually suppressed, brush grows thick and tall. Sooner or later, it burns and takes the tall trees with it. Years of fire suppression have left the forests in a dangerous condition that threatens the lives of firefighters who must battle the raging fires that inevitably erupt. New management practices must be instituted to stop this threat.

Fire is an essential part of most forested ecosystems. Fire recycles forest nutrients, creates browse for native wildlife, deters unwanted noxious weeds, thins out thickets of trees, and rejuvenates forests. Fire creates standing dead trees essential for wood-

Forest Service Employees for Environmental Ethics, "Returning Fire to Our Forest Ecosystems," www.fseee.org, 2002.

peckers and the insects they eat and encourages the growth of native plants.

Fire was the forest management tool of choice for Native Americans for 10,000 years. Frequent burning kept wildlife and the forests they lived in healthy and sustainable. Europeans changed all of that. In many forest ecosystems, such as the dry Ponderosa pine forests, putting out fires has led only to even bigger fires burning when they get out of our control. The Forest Service must rethink its fire policies and we all must learn to live with and manage fire, not fight it.

Current Firefighting Methods Hurt the Environment

Firefighting can be as destructive of the environment as the fire itself. Fire retardant dumped from bombers is toxic to fish if it reaches streams or lakes, just like fertilizer that runs off a farmer's field. Some retardants include cyanide, added to prevent corrosion of bomber tanks. The cyanide adds to the retardant's toxicity. Bulldozers used to clear fire trails disturb soil and increase erosion.

The Forest Service has refused to subject its firefighting activities to the same environmental standards as logging, livestock grazing, and mining. Even building a hiking trail gets more environmental consideration than bulldozing hundreds of miles of fireline. The Clean Water Act requires the Forest Service to get a permit before it dumps fire retardant into a stream. The Endangered Species Act requires the Forest Service to evaluate the effects fire retardant in streams will have on threatened fish. The Forest Service has not complied with either law. . . .

"The Forest Service must rethink its fire policies and we all must learn to live with and manage fire, not fight it."

Fighting fires now accounts for over half of the Forest Service's total budget. But many of these fires should be managed, not fought. Although every forester and ecologist knows that removing fire from forests devastates long-term forest health, the Forest Service still extinguishes over 99 percent of all fires.

The Forest Service refuses to take a hard look at its fire fighting practices. The National Environmental Policy Act requires it does so. . . .

Prevention of Deaths of Forest Firefighters

Firefighters are sometimes sent where they don't belong. In late July 2001, the Forest Service was combating a blaze in an area that should have been allowed to burn. Four young men and women died battling the Thirty Mile fire in the remote Chewuch River canyon of the Okanogan National Forest [in northern Washington]. Tom Craven, Karen Fitzpatrick, Devin Weaver, and Jessica Johnson were sent by the Forest Service to do a job. They died in the performance of that duty.

> *"A century of aggressive fire suppression, combined with logging of the biggest and most fire-resistant trees, has damaged ecosystems throughout the West."*

But was the job they were doing worth their lives? Did this fire, in a steep, remote canyon that threatened no houses or valuable resources, need to be battled? During its investigation into these tragic deaths, the U.S. Forest Service had better answer these questions.

The Thirty Mile fire started in roadless, backcountry land immediately adjacent to the remote Pasayten wilderness. The fire began in a designated Research Natural Area [RNA], at 6,000 acres, one of the largest RNA's in the nation. This is important in what happened next: It appears fire managers did not even know the fire was in a Research Natural Area. Had they known, they would not have aggressively attacked the fire with aerial retardants and firelines, which are banned in RNA's. Instead, they would have held back and taken a more cautious approach to fighting this fire—an approach that sought to allow the fire to mimic natural processes within this fire-dependent ecosystem.

Admittedly, hindsight can be 20-20, but it is worth considering that a more cautious approach to fighting this fire might also have saved lives. The Thirty Mile fire exemplifies the need to take a hard look at our nation's approach to wildland fires.

A century of aggressive fire suppression, combined with logging of the biggest and most fire-resistant trees, has damaged ecosystems throughout the West. Continuing to put out every fire in the remote backcountry makes little sense economically or environmentally. We must carefully restore fire to its prominent role as nature's cleansing agent in our public forests.

In [2001] the Congress allocated a record amount, $1.6 billion, to the Forest Service for its national fire plan. The first priority should be to help private homeowners who live near fire-prone national forests to manage the vegetation within several hundred feet of their houses. That's where the biggest difference is made between a home burning up in a forest fire and a home surviving. The next priority should be to return fire to its natural role in the environment.

Putting out all fires simply puts off the day of reckoning. Burn today or burn tomorrow, the West's forests have burned for thousands of years and will continue to do so. We must learn to live with fire just as we live with the weather. And we must stop sacrificing our best and brightest young people in this futile war against an implacable enemy.

8

Salvage Logging After Wildfires Harms Forest Environments

Timothy Ingalsbee

Timothy Ingalsbee is the director of the Western Fire Ecology Center for the American Lands Alliance, which researches, analyzes, educates, and advocates on fire-related federal forest management issues.

The U.S. Forest Service has a mandate to promote salvage logging in national forests where fires have killed or partially burned large trees. This work is proceeding under the guise of fire prevention because logging companies remove supposedly flammable wood left behind by wildfires. In fact, while it has benefited logging companies, salvage logging will not make forests healthier or safer from wildfires. Worse, salvage logging has been shown to increase fire hazards. In addition, dead or partially burned trees play important roles in the ecology of forests and are necessary for a healthy recovery after a fire. Salvage logging also harms streams, soils, and wildlife. Allowing salvage logging is bad forest management and must be stopped.

Most native species of plants and animals inhabiting forest ecosystems evolved with natural adaptations to the patterns and processes of fire disturbance and recovery. One of the effects of fire disturbances is the creation of dead trees, both standing "snags" and downed logs. Fire-killed snags and logs

Timothy Ingalsbee, PhD, "Salvaging Timber; Scuttling Forests: The Ecological Effects of Post-Fire Salvage Logging," American Lands Alliance's Western Fire Ecology Center, www.americanlands.org/documents/1104945475_salvageimpacts.pdf, 2003. Reproduced by permission.

serve vital roles in the structure and function of healthy forest ecosystems in general, and are especially important for natural recovery processes following fire events. They provide food and shelter to wildlife, fish, and numerous insects, microbes, and fungi that are vital to post-fire recovery and long-term site productivity, they help retard surface water runoff and help retain and build soil, they help cycle nutrients and water to plants and soil, and snags that fall across streams provide links between terrestrial and aquatic ecosystems. Indeed, a forest ecologist could argue that for the sake of healthy wildlife and plant populations, fertile soil, and clean water, large-diameter snags and logs are some of the most valuable trees in the forest.

The vital ecological importance of snags and logs and other "coarse woody debris" (tree trunks and branches greater than three inches in diameter) has only been recognized since the late 1970s. Scientists have learned the vital uses of snags and logs for terrestrial and aquatic species. Unfortunately, the dominant view of forest managers since the 1930s has been that fire-killed trees are a wasted resource unless they are quickly "salvage" logged to extract their economic value for wood products. For decades the U.S. Forest Service and Bureau of Land Management have routinely salvage logged fire-killed trees using predominantly economic arguments, coupled with the assumption that the impacts of salvage logging were less harmful than "green tree" logging because the background effects of forest fires made the impacts of salvage logging relatively insignificant. However, this assumption that post-fire salvage logging causes "no significant effects" should be challenged by the growing weight of scientific evidence that demonstrates that salvage logging exacerbates the short-term adverse effects of fire, causes significant long-term environmental damage and ecological degradation of burned watersheds.

Given that controversy over salvage logging has been growing since the big fires of the late 1980s [such as the one in Yellowstone National Park], some forest managers and elected officials have raised a new justification for salvage logging that capitalizes on the public's socially-conditioned fear of forest fires: the claim that fire-killed trees must be removed quickly before they fuel a future catastrophic wildfire. This is the so-called "reburn hypothesis" and it assumes that fire-killed trees pose an extreme fuel hazard and fire risk; therefore, by removing dead and dying trees, salvage logging can reduce the probability of a future high-intensity wildfire. Unfortunately for the proponents of the reburn hypothesis, there is no support in the scientific literature demonstrating that the probability for high-intensity fires is greater for areas of abundant fire-killed snags and logs compared to salvage logged areas. The fact is, there simply is not a strong scientific or ecological basis for using post-fire salvage logging as a tool for wildfire prevention, post-fire "recovery" objectives, or ecosystem restoration objectives.

On the contrary, a [1995 review by Oregon State University researchers] of the effects of wildfire and salvage came to the conclusion that,

> Human intervention on the post-fire landscape may substantially or completely delay recovery, remove the elements of recovery, or accentuate the damage. . . . In this light, there is little reason to believe that post-fire salvage logging has any positive ecological benefits, particularly for aquatic ecosystems. There is considerable evidence that persistent, significant adverse environmental impacts are likely to result from salvage logging.

They further indicated that, "There is no ecological need for immediate intervention on the post-fire landscape," and advocated that "Human intervention should not be permitted unless and until it is determined that natural recovery processes are not occurring."

The following provides scientific evidence indicating that post-fire salvage logging, far from being an environmentally benign or beneficial management activity, can have significant adverse impacts upon a wide range of forest resources and ecosystem components.

Salvage Logging Causes Significant Effects on Forest Soils

Fires can cause short-term adverse effects on soils such as increasing erosion from removal of vegetative cover that exposes soils to rain and snowfall and subsequent runoff. These impacts vary depending on a number of environmental factors, including the severity of the fire, the steepness of slopes, natural erodibility of soil parent material, precipitation events, and other factors, but in general, burned soils are highly vulnerable to additional disturbance. One of the natural recovery processes initiated by fires is that when large-diameter snags fall to the ground across the slope contour, they serve as natural check-dams that slow runoff and retain soil, which is especially important on steep slopes. Salvage logging directly displaces soils by felling trees and dragging large-diameter logs across the exposed ground surface. But salvage logging also indirectly facilitates erosion through removal of large snags and logs that would have naturally slowed overland flow and retained soil.

In a study that compared five different post-fire salvage logging methods on ponderosa pine sites in eastern Washington, conventional tractor-based systems disturbed nearly 75% of the area, and caused erosion on over 30% of the area, but even helicopter logging caused soil disturbance on 12% of the area. In addition to erosion, salvage logging is also known to cause soil compaction. This also adversely impacts post-fire recovery and long-term site productivity by eliminating pore spaces in soil that retain air, water, and facilitate spread of fine roots. The result of decreased water infiltration and retention is increased surface runoff, sheetwash erosion, and subsequent sedimentation in streams.

> *"For the sake of healthy wildlife and plant populations, fertile soil, and clean water, large-diameter snags and logs are some of the most valuable trees in the forest."*

Salvage logging also causes nutrient losses not only directly through removal of topsoil, but indirectly through the removal of snags and logs. Although most nutrients are stored in foliage and limbs, large logs also function as an important source of soil organic matter and a long-lasting nutrient reservoir for microorganisms, plants, and animals. In fact, in Douglas-fir ecosystems of the Cascade [Mountains], up to 30% or more of upper soil layers are composed of old decayed logs. It can take several centuries, even millennia, for forest soil to develop and become productive. Thus, the problem with soil displacement, compaction, and erosion is that once topsoil has been removed from the ecosystem, it constitutes an irreplaceable loss of fertility and productivity, at least in human timescales. Consequently, protection of the topsoil is a primary requisite for aiding post-fire recovery and maintaining long-term forest ecosystem health.

Salvage Logging Causes Significant Effects on Forest Streams

Fires can affect stream systems through removal of forest litter and duff [matted, decomposed soil] layers which increases erosion and sedimentation, and through changes in peak flows and water yields [into streams]. When vegetation is killed, evapotranspiration is halted; thus, instead of plants taking up water through roots and stems, water remains in soil to flow along slope gradients into streams. Consumption of tree canopies by fire can eliminate their ability to intercept rain and snow, causing increased susceptibility to rainsplash and sheetwash erosion, and snowfall accumulations may experience more rapid spring snowmelt. In some instances, high-severity fires create physical and chemical changes that can cause [water-resistant] soil layers that repel water infiltration, and lead to accelerated overland flow. All of these natural fire-related processes can increase surface water runoff, water yields and peak streamflows, leading to increased potential for erosion, landslides and floods, and subsequent sedimentation of streams. Simple logic as well as empirical research indicates that the net effect of high-severity wildfires is to increase the sensitivity of sites to further soil disturbance.

In the short-term, the adverse effects of high-severity fires—decreased infiltration, increased overland flow, and excess sedimentation in streams—can be greatly exacerbated by the soil disturbance caused by salvage logging. In the long-term, extracting snags that would have become downed logs eliminates their ability to intercept precipitation and retard erosion. Large-diameter logs are also capable of storing vast amounts of water. When logs fall across streams, they trap sediment and form backwater areas and "stair-step" stream profiles that dissipate the energy of flowing water even on high gradient slopes. These check-dams and backwater pools help maintain clean water and create vital resting, feeding, and spawning habitat for aquatic species such as salmon.

Additionally, the interior of large-diameter logs are capable of storing vast amounts of water, releasing water slowly into soil and streams over time, which provides long-lasting, high-moisture [water supplies] that aid forest recovery during drought periods or fires. In a study of downed logs on a dry forest site in the Siskiyou National Forest [in Oregon] that did not have any precipitation for 77 days prior to a high-intensity wildfire, so much water was discovered in the interior of sampled logs that the researchers could literally wring the water out of the wood. A study in the Cascades indicated that decayed logs averaged 350% moisture content in the winter, and 250% in the summer. This water in downed wood aids the establishment of pioneering plants following fire, and maintains adjacent vegetation during drought periods when soil moisture would otherwise be low. Removing large snags and logs by salvage logging eliminates these microhabitats on uplands and can adversely affect water quality and aquatic habitats.

Salvage Logging Causes Significant Effects on Forest Vegetation

Salvage logging can decrease natural plant regeneration, both by mechanical damage from felling and dragging logs across the ground surface, and by changing the microclimate through removing protective shade. The primary effects of removing shade-producing large snags and logs are increased solar radiation causing higher site temperatures and lower relative humidities during daytime, increased heat loss during night, and more extreme temperature fluctuations overall. Soils and vegetation are also more exposed to the drying effects of increased surface winds.

> *"Far from being a 'wasted resource,' large-diameter snags and logs play critical structural and functional roles in maintaining healthy, diverse wildlife populations."*

Even though high-intensity fire may consume tree crowns, the residual shade provided by large-diameter snags and logs is often vital for retaining soil moisture for vulnerable tree seedlings, and for moderating temperature increases in streams for sensitive fish species. For example, on a hypothetical south-facing 50% gradient slope located at 45 degrees latitude, 100 trees averaging 150 feet tall and 24 inches wide would provide 6,900 square feet of shade, or 14% of the slope surface during the course of a day. In an empirical study of headwaters burned by high-intensity wildfire during the 1987 Silver Fire, researchers discovered that dead trees provided 57% of the shade for streams; this was three times more shade than derived by the surrounding topography, and twice as much shade as produced by the remaining live vegetation. In addition to aiding survival of vegetation and fish, the microclimatic effects of shade-producing snags and logs also help mitigate fire hazard. These ecological benefits of fire-killed snags and logs on moderating the microclimate are sacrificed by salvage timber extraction.

Salvage Logging Causes Significant Effects on Wildlife

Although fires can cause mortality of individual animals, in general, wildlife populations often respond positively to fires and in fact are attracted to burns for the flush of nutrients and new vegetation, and the pulse of new snags and logs, that result from fires. Cavity-nesting species are prime beneficiaries of fires, and 62 species of birds and mammals use snags, broken-topped, diseased or otherwise "defective" trees for roosting, denning, foraging, or other life functions. In the Douglas-fir region of western Oregon, approximately 20% (34 species) of all bird species depend on snags for nesting for foraging. In bird studies conducted in the Foothills and Star Gulch Fires, 87 bird species were recorded in the burns, 43 species built nests, and 67% of those species were neotropical migrants. In another field study, 96% of all dead trees within monitoring plots showed evidence of foraging by woodpeckers within one year after the fire. Woodpeckers are an especially important species, since they excavate cavities essential for non-excavating species such as bats and squirrels. Recent studies indicate that current management guidelines for maintaining snag density may be too low to provide for desired population levels of woodpeckers because the guidelines only focus on their nesting requirements.

Relatively large diameter trees (e.g., greater than 20 inches DBH [diameter at breast height]) are not only more utilized by cavity-nesting wildlife, but they also stand longer and have greater longevity as downed logs than smaller-diameter trees. Large-diameter trees enable bigger cavities for larger-sized animals, and the deep furrows of their bark provide greater food supply of insects. In addition to snags, large-diameter logs are utilized for feeding, shelter, and reproduction by a number of mammals, reptiles, amphibians, and insects. The density and distribution of snags and logs in Douglas-fir forest ecosystems greatly influences the density and distribution of snag/log-dependent wildlife. Empirical studies have found that the range of snag diameters, and average length and frequency of downed logs in streams was greatest in unmanaged old-growth stands compared to salvage-logged areas. In fact, forest managers are finding it difficult to meet the number, density, size, and condition of snags required by their Forest Plans due to past salvage logging and old-growth clearcutting that removed snags.

Far from being a "wasted resource," large-diameter snags and logs play critical structural and functional roles in maintaining healthy, diverse wildlife populations. Indeed, an ecologist could argue that a dead tree sustains more wildlife than a live tree. However, salvage logging primarily targets larger-diameter trees because they typically represent a relatively high commercial value.

Salvage Logging Can Increase Fire Risks and Fuel Hazards

Salvage logging proponents may acknowledge the essential ecological roles and values that snags and logs provide for soils, streams, vegetation, and wildlife, but these values may be negated because of a desire to reduce fire risks and fuel hazards. However, as previously noted, there are no scientific studies demonstrating that large-diameter fire-killed snags pose an increased risk of high-intensity reburns, or that salvage logging effectively reduces fire risk. On the contrary, there is growing scientific evidence that large-diameter snags and logs have naturally low flammability while post-fire salvage logging itself may actually increase the rate of spread, intensity, and severity of fires.

Large snags are important ignition sources during lightning storms, but from the standpoint of the physics of combustion, it is the fine fuels such as grass, needles, and small limbs that carry fire, not large dead woody material. Large-diameter fuels have naturally low flammability because they have a low surface-area-to-volume ratio (SAVR) that limits the amount of oxygen available for combustion. Conversely, smaller fuel particles have higher SAVR values which fuel higher rates of spread and fireline intensity. Consequently, only dead fuels less than three inches in diameter and live fuels less than ¼ inch in diameter are used in fire spread models because it is these fine fuels that propagate fire; large-diameter fuels (greater than three inches in diameter) are not included in the calculations for fire spread at all. Furthermore, large-diameter fuels retain moisture longer and later into the season, further reducing their flammability particularly when wildfire potential is at its greatest.

> *"Given these environmental impacts and ecological tradeoffs, the claim that salvage logging is a valid tool for forest recovery, rehabilitation, or restoration must be challenged."*

Large standing tree boles [trunks], dead or alive, are typically unavailable for combustion especially when fires have removed underlying ground vegetation and downed fuels. While dead trees may be more flammable for 2–3 years after a fire while their dead needles are retained, after their needles drop to the ground, crown fire hazard essentially drops to zero, and the standing tree boles do not readily ignite. Most larger tree boles are not consumed by fire even if killed, and then they often remain standing for decades, providing biological legacy and ecological values essential for natural post-fire recovery processes. When snags fall to the ground then their relative flammability increases, but it may take as long as 20 years for a pulse of burned ponderosa pine trees 6–9 inches DBH to fall, and recent research suggests that larger ponderosa pine trees can remain standing up to 80 years. Large-diameter downed logs in isolation do not burn well, if at all, unless they are very dry and placed in close proximity to each other (approximately two tree diameters apart). On the other hand, well decayed logs can burn easily via glowing combustion, but this does not cause extreme fire behavior. Decayed logs can smolder for long periods of time, causing high severity, but these effects are localized to underlying and adjacent soil. Snags and logs can emit burning embers that if lifted by wind can cause spotfires, but these embers can only ignite in fine fuels, not other large snags or logs. The low flammability of large-diameter downed logs is further mitigated by their interior water content which increases with the length of time they are on the forest floor and their subsequent stage of decay.

Salvage logging typically removes the larger diameter trees that have the most commercial value but least flammability, but leaves behind the smaller diameter trees and logging slash that have little to no commercial value but are the most flammable fuels. In calculating the fire hazard of slash-laden salvage logging units, they are assigned fuel model 12, one of the highest ratings for rapid fire spread and fireline intensity. Indeed, in a study modeling the effects of various fuels treatments in the Sierra Nevada, lop-and-scatter, group selection (small clearcuts), and salvage logging operations that left the slash and adjacent landscape untreated produced the highest fireline intensity, heat per unit area, rate of spread, area burned, and scorch height of all other fuels method treatments because they increased the flammable surface fuel load. The researcher concluded that salvage logging would make the fire situation more severe because removing only large, standing trees will not reduce fire hazard in Sierra Nevada forest ecosystems. The same principles of fire physics contrasting the flammability of large-diameter logs versus small-diameter salvage logging slash applies to other ecosystems and regions, as well.

Fire-created snags and logs serve many vital ecological functions for forest soils, streams, vegetation, and wildlife. Large-diameter snags and logs can also help mitigate conditions that lead to high-intensity fires, and aid post-fire natural recovery processes. Conversely, commercially extracting fire-killed trees via salvage logging causes significant short- and long-term adverse effects on forest ecosystem structures, functions and processes. Considering the wide array of vital ecological services that snags and logs provide, the term "salvage" is appropriate only for logging operations in which the primary management objective is extraction of commodity timber values at the expense of other economic and ecological values. Given these environmental impacts and ecological tradeoffs, the claim that salvage logging is a valid tool for forest recovery, rehabilitation, or restoration must be challenged. The more scientists learn about the ecological values of large fire-killed snags and logs, the more clear it becomes that "salvaging" burned trees is scuttling forest ecosystems.

9

Logging in Tongass National Forest Shows Forest Management at Its Worst

Leonie Sherman

Leonie Sherman is a freelance writer and radio reporter who specializes in environmental issues.

While logging is being slowed or halted in many national forests, the plan to log the unique temperate rain forests of the Tongass National Forest in Alaska proceeds at full speed. Although extensive scientific studies call for the Tongass to be preserved, corporations and the U.S. Forest Service plan to build thousands of miles of logging roads through some of the most environmentally sensitive forests in the world. The plan to cut down hundreds of thousands of ancient trees to make plywood is not only a crime against the environment but it makes no economic sense. Logging will only provide a few hundred jobs and a global lumber glut has caused wood prices to plummet. In addition, logging will seriously harm the tourist, recreation, and salmon industries that generate tens of thousands of jobs in Alaska. The U.S. Forest Service and some Alaska politicians are beholden to big business and are going to destroy an irreplaceable environmental treasure.

On December 23 [2003], approximately 6:00 P.M. Eastern Standard Time, staffers at the US Forest Service in Washington, DC pressed the "send" buttons on their fax machines, then scuttled through their office doors before the telephones started ringing.

They were apparently hoping that the nation would be too preoccupied with loved ones and [Christmas] celebrations to notice that the largest national forest in America had just been placed on the chopping block. The press releases they sent nationwide announced that Alaska's Tongass National Forest was now exempt from the Roadless Rule.

The Clinton-era Roadless Rule was intended to preserve those roadless areas larger than 7,500 acres not already protected by other legislation. Of the 58 million acres protected by the rule, 9.8 million, or about one sixth, were in the Tongass.

Former Alaskan governor Tony Knowles filed a lawsuit on behalf of the state before the ink from Clinton's signature was dry. He alleged that a clause in ANILCA—the Alaska National Interest Land Conservation Act of 1980, which resulted in the preservation of 115 million acres—decreed that no more land could be protected in the state. The decision to exempt the Tongass from the Roadless Rule is the result of an out-of-court settlement of the lawsuit that was carried forth by Alaska's current governor, Frank Murkowski.

> *"Last year [in 2003] the Forest Service spent over 35 million dollars of taxpayer money to support less than 200 jobs in the Tongass."*

The past 13 years have seen a flurry of paperwork and litigation pertaining to the Tongass, culminating in a 49-day public comment period this past summer [2003]. The Forest Service received an impressive total of roughly 133,000 public comments, or an average of 2,715 a day.

The US Forest Service does not track how many comments are in favor of the Tongass's continued protection by the Roadless Rule, according to Ray Massey, public affairs specialist for Alaska Region's National Forests. "This is not a vote," Massey says. "Let's say we got 100,000 comments from people who want the Tongass to remain protected by the Roadless Rule. Well, unless they present new scientific information we haven't seen in previous Environmental Impact Statements, then they're not much use to us."

Dennis Neill, public affairs specialist for the Tongass National Forest, was hard-pressed to cite any scientific evidence that supports removing the Tongass from the Roadless Rule. The last extensive scientific study of the Tongass was performed in 1997, and Neill admits that since that time, "we have not undertaken any specific scientific study or experiments." Over 300 North American scientists, 100 of them from Alaska, supported protecting the Tongass under the Roadless Rule.

Open Season on the Trees

"This decision is a slap in the face to both sound science and the public interest," insists John Shane, senior scientist for Audubon Alaska and a field biologist who worked for 12 years in the Tongass National Forest. "The Roadless Rule would have safeguarded the integrity of the Tongass forest and would have ensured the sustainable use of fish, wildlife, and recreational resources in perpetuity," Shane said. According to Shane, the Tongass is "one of the few places in the US where we have an opportunity to protect intact, functional ecosystems which still include healthy populations of wolves, brown bears, bald eagles, and five species of Pacific salmon."

Much of the 9.8 million acres opened up by this recent decision is rock, ice, and muskeg. But the "heart of the Tongass" has timber companies drooling—300,000 acres of high-volume old-growth timber situated in low-elevation valleys. Only 676,000 acres of the Tongass contains such valuable timber. Most of the 376,000 acres of old growth previously unprotected from road building and clear-cutting has already been depleted for pulp. Now it's open season on the remaining 300,000 acres.

The rationale behind this ruling is that it will create jobs. Southeast Alaska undoubtedly needs jobs. Fishermen are hocking their boats and permits as they face a world market glutted with farmed fish. All the easily accessible minerals have been stripped from the land. Logging has never been profitable in the Tongass, though government subsidized pulp mills in Ketchikan and Sitka employed people for about 30 years. Those went out of business in the late 1990s; even with a generous federal subsidy they couldn't compete on the world market.

But exempting the Tongass from the Roadless Rule will create only a small number of jobs in the southeast, as the area does not have the capacity to process the timber locally. Spruce and hemlock will be shipped south to be transformed into railroad ties and plywood, and the yellow cedar will be exported as raw logs to Japan.

"Last year [in 2003] the Forest Service spent over 35 million dollars of taxpayer money to support less than 200 jobs in the Tongass," said Buck Lindkugel, staff attorney and conservation director for the Southeast Alaska Conservation Council. Alaska's own economists have concluded that Tongass timber is no longer competitive in world markets.

Despite setbacks in recent years due to the introduction of cheap farmed fish, commercial fishing is still the largest private employer in southeast Alaska. Ninety percent of the salmon that are the backbone of this industry are born in the lakes and streams of the Tongass. Opening up the Tongass to road building and clear-cutting will have disastrous consequences on the salmon runs that people rely on for their subsistence and livelihoods.

Alaska's fishermen get cash bailouts. Why not give loggers cash and let the rest of us keep the forest?

The only sector of southeast Alaska's economy that shows consistent growth in recent years is tourism. Tourists come to Alaska from all over the world because it is one of the last truly wild places on the planet. Cruise ships ply the Inside Passage [the waterway near Alaska's shore], carrying as many as 750,000 passengers in a four month season. The experience of passing endless green islands, viewing wildlife on the land and in the water, is what brings tourists to southeast Alaska. They don't come to see roads and clear-cuts.

The Tongass National Forest covers 16.8 million acres, by far the largest in America's national forest system. It's the largest intact coastal temperate rainforest on the planet. Not just a state treasure or even a federal jewel, the Tongass represents habitat of global significance.

Marbled murrelets, Queen Charlotte goshawks, and bald eagles soar over these emerald isles. Sitka black-tailed deer, brown bears, and wolverines slink among the towering trees. Orcas, humpback whales, and Stellar sea lions create a ruckus just offshore. All five species of Pacific salmon thrive in this wild, wet wonderland. Humans depend on the wild animals and plants for their subsistence and have done so for countless generations.

The Tongass National Forest belongs to all Americans, and we share responsibility for its management. Removing the Tongass from the Roadless Rule was a setback, but as [writer] Alice Walker reminds us, "anything we love can be saved."

10

Religious Leaders Call for an End to Commercial Logging on Public Lands

Religious Campaign for Forest Conservation

The Religious Campaign for Forest Conservation is an organization made up of over two hundred prominent biologists and scientists whose goals include ending all clearing of old-growth forests and stopping commercial logging on public land.

Protecting the wilderness is a sacred religious duty. Trees and pristine forests are creations of God and cannot be destroyed for economic profit without degrading society and its religious heritage. According to the Judeo-Christian values upon which America was founded, forests should be managed to protect all life on the planet for generations to come. The Bible depicts trees as symbols of life, stability, fruitfulness, and integrity. Therefore, commercial logging of these trees must be stopped.

Editor's Note: The following selection is an extract of a letter the Religious Campaign for Forest Conservation addressed to President Bush in 2004, calling upon him to stop commercial logging on public lands.

Over the past several years, numerous religious organizations have issued declarations on forest conservation. This

Religious Campaign for Forest Conservation, "Open Letter to the President from America's Religious Leaders," http://creationethics.org, February 3, 2004.

is because issues of forest conservation at their core are also religious issues. They are religious issues because God commands care of creation and because trees anchor the life support system of the planet. For Christians and Jews alike the biblical story of human interaction with the world begins with God's commands regarding two trees. The way those first people responded reflected their relationship to their Creator and their fidelity to the commands given to them.

Judaism and Christianity teach that we share a sacred obligation to God and future generations to protect and safeguard the biological systems that sustain humanity and the vitality of the planet. As a people we have been given dominion over Earth and commanded to steward its air, land and water. We are obliged to care for creation and ensure the fruitfulness and integrity of the biological processes that are essential for the life of the planet. These biblical commands provide a vision for humanity to dwell in harmony with God and the land. It is our human task to "dress and keep" creation and function in harmony with this ancient vision.

The way we interact with forests and all of God's creation is thus informed by religious teaching. Yet this vision of human purpose has faded in our nation's public policy. Not only are the great forests of the world disappearing, in our own country, barely 4% of America's original great forest remains.

The irony of this predicament is that the forests that are being lost to commercial logging are more valuable if left standing than when cut for lumber or pulp. Studies show that forest conservation brings important economic and social values. A 1995 U.S. Forest Service report found that there are many more rural jobs and more rural income when the forests are preserved. Opinion polls reflect that 70% of Americans would save the national forests from commercial logging. The clear fact is the forests have spiritual, biological and social values far in excess of their dollar or commodity values.

Places of Inspiration and Beauty

To people of faith, forests are places of inspiration and beauty. They witness to the power and majesty of God. Forests also reflect a unique handiwork of the Creator that reconnects us to the wonder and mystery of creation. To people of science, forests are "the lungs of the planet" and repositories of medicines and undiscovered cures for disease. Intact forest systems provide an array of natural services: They provide clean air and clean water. They metabolize carbon dioxide, restraining global climate change, releasing oxygen and sequestering carbon dioxide. They inhibit catastrophic fires. They serve social stability by regulating stream flows, transpiring moisture to enhance rainfall and restraining hillsides from erosion. They offer habitat for animal and plant species, many of them endangered. They afford recreation by providing places for hunting and fishing, hiking and camping, and many forms of outdoor repast and respite from the hurried and harried pace of society.

> *"The forests that are being lost to commercial logging are more valuable if left standing than when cut for lumber or pulp."*

The severe wildfires that our country recently experienced should call attention to the failures of past forest policies. The combination of excessive fuel loads caused by suppressing small fires, the flammable "slash" debris left by logging, the drying of the forests caused by removal of the largest trees—which are also the most fire resistant, coupled with record drought in many parts of the nation, have resulted in predictably higher levels of catastrophic fire damage. Because commercial logging degraded and dried the national forests, there can be no sounder policy than to end the roadbuilding and logging that have bequeathed us this unnecessary fire hazard and to institute a policy of ending commercial logging on the national forests.

Numerous religious organizations have studied the array of forest concerns and issued formal statements. Roman Catholic Franciscans, Episcopalians, Evangelical Christians, Jewish organizations, the United Methodist Church and many others have national or regional declarations calling for an end to commercial logging on the national forests.

These statements are emerging because forest issues are issues of value. Former U.S. Forest Service Chief Max Peterson recently related that after all the studies are done, "the problems facing our forests are not technical or scientific questions, they are value questions." Because forest questions at heart are questions of values and principles, the voice of religion has a responsibility to address this issue.

Mr. President, on behalf of the churches and synagogues of America, we appeal to your religious sensitivity and particularly to your campaign promise that you would apply religious principle to the policies of your administration. Please listen to the voice of the religious leaders who are calling for an end to commercial logging on the national forests. Please listen to the voice of science, which has called for this same end. Please listen to the majority of Americans, 70% of whom wish to end commercial logging on the national forests. Listen to us all as we ask you to stand up for religion, morality, right reason, unbiased science and a large majority of the American people. Stop the commercial logging of our national forests.

11

Local Communities Should Manage Their Own Forests

Jane Braxton Little

Jane Braxton Little is an environmental journalist based in Greenville, California.

Rural planners and forest workers often possess intimate knowledge of their local woodlands. Local community forest projects have taken advantage of this knowledge to successfully restore damaged ecosystems, remove abandoned roads, and thin brush to reduce fire danger. Unfortunately, Forest Service bureaucracy, a lack of funding from Congress, and environmentalist opposition often stands in the way of expanding these programs. With rampant unemployment in many forest communities, the Forest Service should support these stewardship projects to benefit the environment, the community, and the regional economy.

George Ramirez tugs at his hat, grips the edge of a podium, and faces a crowd of U.S. Forest Service officials in a downtown Washington, DC, conference room. This is unfamiliar territory for Ramirez, a woodcutter and rancher from rural New Mexico. He has come to report to the federal agency for Las Humanas, a cooperative of land grant villages. More than 100 members . . . completed a 16-acre thinning project on the Cibola National Forest [in the summer of 2000].

"We showed we have the labor force and the skills to im-

Jane Braxton Little, "Stewardship's Trial by Forests," *American Forests*, vol. 106, Autumn 2000, p. 49.

prove the forest," he says. "It gives a lot of pride in our community to do this work."

New partnerships are bringing people like Ramirez to the nation's capital arm driving the Forest Service into innovations on national forests from Oregon to New Hampshire. The projects are transforming the type of work done on federal lands, how it is done, and who does it.

Some call this new approach to forest management collaborative stewardship, others call it stewardship contracting or ecosystem management. By any name, the changes hold promise—for the forests and for the communities surrounded by national forests. At a time when federal land managers are shifting their objectives from commercial logging to restoring ecosystems, these stewardship projects test new strategies for managing the woods and new systems for contracting the work. Instead of focusing on what's removed from the forest, they focus on what is left.

> *"Successful projects require enormous cooperation and creativity to incorporate nontraditional activities into a rigid bureaucratic system."*

For the rural communities that have advocated a greater role in forest management decisions, the stewardship projects represent a major milestone. After nearly a decade of campaigning for work that improves the national forests in their backyards and provides local jobs, they now boast a variety of on-the-ground projects with tangible results. In addition to Ramirez's Las Humanas thinning project in New Mexico, a coalition in Swan Valley, Montana, has harvested small trees from three different forests stands where they plan to use prescribed burning to maintain the natural spacing. In southwestern Colorado, the Ponderosa Pine Forest Partnership combined thinning and slash removal on 450 acres to test whether it could market and make a profit from small-diameter trees.

Compared to the multimillion board-feet timber sales of the past, these stewardship projects are minuscule. They involve little commercial logging, use local labor, and emphasize restoration. Although Forest Service officials recognize that the era of clearcutting and industrial timber sales has waned, many hesitate to embrace the innovations proposed by community groups. Even enthusiastic proponents involved in developing the proposals have struggled to fit unfamiliar and unconventional activities into everyday government rounds.

An Innovative Approach

Successful projects require enormous cooperation and creativity to incorporate nontraditional activities into a rigid bureaucratic system. They depend on the ideas and entrepreneurial skills of civic and timber industry leaders, woods workers, and state and federal officials. Working together, these partners have developed novel solutions for problems that once seemed impossible.

"Local people can do some good things for the forest. And the restoration work gives us a shot at restoring these small economies."

One of the most stubborn issues has been how to pay contractors for their restoration work. Historically, the Forest Service has funded thinning, tree planting, and other forest rehabilitation through timber sales. Stewardship projects typically produce no commercial sawlogs, which leaves the agency with no funding mechanism. A community coalition in northwestern Montana came up with a one-time solution to demonstrate the effects of restoring 112 acres of the Flathead National Forest to a patchwork of old-growth and younger trees. The Cedar Flats project involved some logging but the contractor was hired primarily to improve the woods, not harvest timber, says Carol Daly, president of the Flathead Economic Policy Center in Montana. Left with no way to pay for his services, the coalition raised $120,000 in foundation funds, a system Daly calls "forestry by bake sale."

Other dilemmas that community groups and Forest Service officials encounter involve bundling several different jobs into one contract and extending contracts over several years to make the work economically feasible. Thinning, road removal, and stream restoration, for example, historically have been separate contracts issued by separate Forest Service branches. Most of these service contracts have required completion within a year.

As the number of proposals for stewardship forestry has grown and pressure from communities increased, Forest Service officials have felt compelled to respond.

Some of the projects are nontraditional but permissible under existing law. Others seemed worth trying but clearly do not comply with current federal regulations.

Twenty-eight Pilot Projects

In 1998 the Forest Service turned to Capitol Hill for help. Late that year Congress approved legislation directing the agency to implement 28 pilot projects that would test contracting and funding mechanisms not authorized by government statutes. These stewardship pilot projects ranged from creating a high-elevation habitat for neotropical birds in Tennessee to an Idaho project that uses logging and prescribed burns to restore elk habitat along the Clearwater River. Several demonstrate ways to improve the use of local workers' skill and knowledge. Others test new methods of harvesting timber and new ways to pay for it. All the demonstration projects require monitoring by agencies and individuals, in addition to using evaluators from a variety of perspectives, this experiment in monitoring will test the collaborative approach to gathering scientific data.

> *"We do a successful project and we're supposed to go back to starving? I can't figure out why we have to struggle and beg when we produce a success."*

The legislation represents "a big giant step" toward legitimizing community-based forestry within the Forest Service and beyond, says Lynn, chair of the Seventh American Forest Congress Communities Committee. "There's hope, some belief that local people can do some good things for the forest. And the restoration work gives us a shot at restoring these small economies," she says.

But recognition of the role communities play in national forest management has been slow to move from Washington,

DC, to the ground, and it has not always brought material results. The forest thinning done on the Cibola Forest by Las Humanas is one of the few Forest Service–sponsored stewardship projects completed in the 18 months since the legislation was adopted. In fact, it is one of the few for which work has even started. Most are mired in bureaucracy, their sponsors struggling to get them out of discussion and onto the ground.

Bureaucratic Hurdles

So if everyone thinks they're a good idea, what's blocking the projects? In short, a dearth of funds and a federal agency uncertain of its mandate and its mission. Forest stewardship projects also face opposition from environmentalists who fear they are often little more than timber sales masquerading as forest restoration projects.

Cliff Hickman, a Forest Service official who coordinates the stewardship projects from the national office, puts some of the blame on the controversy that surrounds the agency's every action. How contractors are paid and what happens to the money are issues hotly disputed even in demonstration projects, he says.

Controversy has contributed to the funding problems that have plagued the stewardship pilots since Congress approved them. The legislators awarded no money for work [in 1999] and halved the Forest Service's request for [2000]. Several projects have been delayed because local district officials do not have the money to pay for required environmental studies. . . .

Along with funding, he acknowledges that confusion within the Forest Service has helped stall implementation of the pilot projects. Communication is sometimes poor and anything "new and different from the traditional" causes some Forest Service officials to balk, Hickman says. Many of the experiments in stewardship combine timber sales and service contracts, functions that have historically been handled by different branches within the agency. Others require negotiations with groups new to the Forest Service and to government contracting. . . .

The delays are frustrating to Ramirez, chairman of the Las Humanas Cooperative. Working on the Cibola Forest project showed that his community can overcome its historic unemployment—sometimes as high as 45 percent—and produce workers with skills to do thinning that improves the health of the forest. In exchange for their labor, available mostly on weekends, Las Humanas members kept the trees they cut. Some of the material was used for firewood and some for traditional fencing and viga poles used in southwestern houses.

"The Forest Service always said they had no dependable workers. We always said it was because there are no dependable jobs. We broke that cycle," says Ramirez.

Now Las Humanas wants to turn this labor force onto 5,000 acres of federal land in the nearby Estancia Basin. The valley southeast of Albuquerque is a critical water recharge area in desperate need of attention. Las Humanas plans to return the basin to a more natural state by thinning some sections, fencing cattle out of others, and leaving large islands undisturbed for wildlife. The missing ingredient: money.

"It's very aggravating," Ramirez says. "We do a successful project and we're supposed to go back to starving? I can't figure out why we have to struggle and beg when we produce a success."

Other Hurdles

Elsewhere the hurdles for stewardship forestry are even more daunting. The Grassy Flats project near Hayfork, California, was designed to remove small-diameter trees from fire-prone thickets to test the effect on forest health. Local business owners also wanted to test the economic feasibility of milling these 10-inch diameter trees for furniture, flooring and other finished products.

The project was poised for a promising start. Local entrepreneurs had already built and tested special equipment to handle the logs without damaging other trees or the forest floor. Loggers had thinned 40 acres of Trinity National Forest nearby and were ready to move onto the 270-acre Grassy Flats area when a federal court ruling brought everything to a standstill. According to the ruling, before the Forest Service can do anything that disturbs the ground, it must first complete a series of federally mandated surveys of mollusks and 235 other species.

Although local crews were trained and set to do the survey work, they could not afford to wait while the Forest Service completed the paperwork, says the Communities Committee's Jungwirth, who is also executive director of the Watershed Research and Training Center in Hayfork. This spring [2000] Forest Service hired a Canadian firm to survey the Trinity Forest for mollusks.

Using out-of-area crews is a familiar and discouraging trend, says Jungwirth. From 1990 to 1997 local workers captured a meager 6 percent of the more than $1 million of service work contracted annually in the national forest. Now they are seeing restoration work go to outside workers, too. That threatens the critical link between forests and communities, Jungwirth says.

"We know what happened to our communities when we were colonized by big companies around timber. How are we not going to recolonize rural communities around biodiversity?" she says.

Most Projects Utilize Logging

Environmentalists have been watching the stewardship program with a wariness that ranges from distrust to outright opposition. The National Audubon Society welcomes the emphasis on forest restoration but is concerned about including any commercial timber sales—even small ones—in stewardship contracts. A system that allows contractors to keep logs in exchange for removing them provides an incentive to take more timber than may be good for the forest, says Michael T. Leahy, Audubon's forest campaign director.

All but two of the 28 pilot projects include some form of logging. Although they are generally small and do not use traditional timber sale methods, cutting any trees for lumber fuels environmentalists' suspicion that stewardship contracting is little more than a mask for commercial timber harvesting, says Steve Holmer, campaign coordinator for American Lands Alliance. The Forest Service may have heightened those suspicions when Anne Bartuska, director of national forest timber management, told a Senate subcommittee that stewardship contracting is the future of the agency's timber sale program.

Giving loggers the timber they remove in exchange for the service they perform is not an improvement, Holmer says. "The notion that the Forest Service will stop selling trees in timber sales and instead start just giving them away as part of stewardship contracts is a huge step in the wrong direction."

What many urban-based environmentalists overlook is the deep bond between communities and the health of the national forests that surround their small towns, says Jungwirth. Rural coalitions don't want a return to the days of big-volume timber sales, when they watched log trucks roll bumper to bumper down Main Street, exporting more logs out of town than even the loggers thought prudent. They also don't want a return to the 1990s, when some of their neighbors left their families at home for out-of-town jobs while others paraded down Main Street in moving vans and left town altogether.

If they can survive this experimental phase and usher in stewardship forestry as a permanent Forest Service program, rural leaders believe both their communities and the woods will be better off. Stewardship forestry can restore national forests and create high-skilled living-pay jobs "so dads can sleep at home at night," says Jungwirth.

For Ramirez, that means fewer trips to DC. For his rural New Mexico community, it could mean an end to 45 percent unemployment. "Things are changing," says Ramirez. "They've already changed for us. Maybe this can work all over this country."

12

The U.S. Forest Service Needs to Preserve Roadless Areas

Kim Davitt

Kim Davitt is a naturalist, researcher, and conservation advocate for American Wildlands, a conservation organization in the northern Rocky Mountains. She has also served as the cochair of the Headwaters Group of the Sierra Club.

The debate over building roads in 60 million acres of national forest has been intense since Bill Clinton signed the Roadless Area Conservation Rule in the last days of his presidency. In 2004 the George W. Bush administration considerably weakened the rule, allowing state governments to decide which areas should remain roadless. While judges, environmentalists, and politicians argue over the rule, evidence shows that roads harm valuable forest ecosystems in a myriad of ways. Roads and the resulting invasion of trucks, off-road vehicles, and other motorized traffic harms endangered species, increases erosion, and threatens streams. While logging companies are eager for taxpayers to finance expensive roads through roadless areas so they can log old-growth timber, forest managers need to preserve these American treasures in their natural, pristine state.

There are few areas in the United States that you can not access with a motor vehicle. We are an automotive society and roads will take us nearly everywhere that we want. The open road has come to symbolize American freedom, indepen-

Kim Davitt, "Roadless Areas in the Northern Rockies: What We Have Lost Since the Forest Plans," http://wildlands.org, August 18, 2004.

dence, and escape. For many conservationists, these roads also symbolize water pollution via sedimentation, forest fragmentation, and a loss of wildlife habitat. There are currently over 377,000 miles of roads on America's National Forests—eight times the combined length of the interstate highway system. Yet there are a few strongholds of land left which can not be accessed by the automobile. Fewer still can not be accessed by off-road vehicles or motorbikes. Lands without roads and without cars are called roadless areas, an important resource that is rapidly diminishing.

"There are currently over 377,000 miles of roads on America's National Forests—eight times the combined length of the interstate highway system."

Within roadless areas, people do not dominate the landscape. Roadless areas on public land include designated Wilderness [Areas], Wilderness Study Areas, Inventoried Roadless Areas (IRAs), and uninventoried roadless lands. Because these lands are not easily accessible to the logging truck or bulldozer, the forests remain relatively intact. Roadless areas contain some of our only remaining wild forests. In the Western United States, National Forests keep an inventory of large blocks of unroaded land, which are at least 5,000 acres in size and have received very little human development. Uninventoried roadless lands either do not fit the 5,000 acre size requirement or have not yet been added to the formal inventory. One-third of the nation's roadless lands, nearly 20 million acres, are located in the Northern Rockies of Idaho (9.3 million acres), Montana (6.4 million acres) and Wyoming (3.3 million acres).

What Is a Roadless Area?

The Roadless Area Review and Evaluation (RARE I) conducted the first inventory of roadless lands which were not designated in the 1964 Wilderness Act. Between 1971 and 1973, the Forest Service reviewed 56 million acres of roadless areas larger than 5,000 acres on National Forests. . . . This review was deemed insufficient by most proponents of wilderness. In 1979, the Forest

Service completed a second attempt to review roadless areas, called RARE II. Of the 62 million acres inventoried in the study, 15 million were recommended for Wilderness designation, 12 million for further consideration of their wilderness potential, and 36 million for non-Wilderness uses. RARE II was criticized for its incomplete information and its bias toward development. This inventory has been used as a starting point for making Wilderness designation and served as a basis for over twenty Wilderness bills in the early 1980s. Yet there are many areas from the RARE II study that have not been designated Wilderness; these areas have been incorporated into each National Forest's Forest Plan roadless inventory and serve as additional lands for potential Wilderness. In their own right, these National Forest roadless areas are important for clean water, high quality fish and wildlife habitat, quiet back-country recreation, and beautiful scenery, regardless of whether or not they have been designated for inclusion into Wilderness Area protection.

Roadless Area Losses

The Forest Service estimates that there are roughly 58.5 million acres of unprotected, inventoried roadless lands left in the country. There are also millions of acres of uninventoried roadless lands on our public lands. Many of these roadless lands have been developed since Forest Plans were created for National Forests in the mid-1980s. In the Northern Rockies, over 440,000 acres of inventoried roadless areas have been destroyed as a result of timber harvest, road building, and other development since the Forest planning process began. Idaho received the largest amount of roadless destruction—over 320,000 acres from seven National Forests. On ten National Forests in Montana, the Forest Service developed approximately 112,000 acres of inventoried roadless lands. Wyoming National Forests have failed to track their roadless development; a minimum of nearly 10,000 acres has been destroyed on two National Forests.

Additional acres have been lost from the Forest Service inventory due to re-mapping efforts on many of the National Forests. Much of the remaining roadless areas are threatened by current and future development projects such as logging. With many of the roaded forest lands already cut, the timber industry and the Forest Service are looking to roadless areas to provide large, mature trees for timber harvesting. The emergency salvage rider of the 1995 Recissions Act [the act exempted salvage timber sales from being restricted by environmental review] provided justification to log and develop our last wild places. A prolific number of logging proposals were developed under the Emergency Salvage Program which severed public trust with the agency. In response to this breach of trust, former Forest Service Chief Michael Dombeck told Congress in February of 1997, "The unfortunate reality is that many people presently do not trust us to do the right thing. Until we rebuild that trust and strengthen those relationships, it is simply common sense that we avoid [logging in] riparian, old growth and roadless areas."

> *"National Forest roadless areas are important for clean water, high quality fish and wildlife habitat, quiet back-country recreation, and beautiful scenery."*

In January, 2001, the Clinton Administration issued the Roadless Area Conservation Rule to limit logging and development in nearly 60 million acres of inventoried roadless lands on the U.S. National Forest. [More] recently, in July, 2004, the Bush Administration announced a proposal for a new Roadless Rule that removes many of the protections in the original rule and opens up these irreplaceable roadless areas to road-building and resource extraction. Roadless lands are a limited resource in the Northern Rockies and these rule changes are probably the greatest threat to wildlife habitat, clean water, and fisheries in the region.

The development of 440,000 acres of roadless lands since the Forest Planning process in the Northern Rockies is a gross underestimation. The USFS [U.S. Forest Service] simply has not done its job in monitoring the diminution of this resource.

In Wyoming, for example, National Forests have interpreted the 1984 Wyoming Wilderness Act as directing them to ignore their roadless inventory until Forest Plans are revised. . . . Such an assumption violates federal laws which require Forests to disclose a project's irretrievable impacts on roadless resources and to monitor this important resource. . . . The result of their former roadless monitoring failure . . . is that the three Wyoming forests . . . can not report how many acres of inventoried roadless lands have been developed. . . . Clearly, we do not know the extent of roadless area development in Wyoming for the past decade as a result of their misinterpretation of the release language in the Act. . . .

Forest Service technology related to land management tracking has improved in the last few years and on many National Forests. These new technical capabilities have given clearer pictures of roadless inventories. However, many Forests are not yet using new computer technologies such as Geographical Information Systems (GIS) and Landsat images. A study by The Wilderness Society (TWS) reveals that much of the Forest Service's information is incomplete and grossly underestimated. . . . Thus, the Forest Service's number of approximately 440,000 developed acres is extremely conservative. The continued loss of these wildlands will have severe impacts on the ecology and economy of the Northern Rockies region.

Ecological Importance

The Forest Service and Bureau of Land Management have contributed a significant number of reports regarding the ecological importance of roadless areas. Forest Service Chiefs and Supervisors have spoken publicly about the high quality wildlife and fish habitat inherent in undisturbed, roadless forests. Yet, the management direction and actions taken by this same agency's line-officers contradicts higher-ranking managers' speeches and studies. While acknowledging the ecological importance of roadless areas, the Forest Service directly destroys beneficial roadless characteristics via timber sales, road building projects, oil and gas development, and other extractive resource projects.

As the Forest Service stated in the Roadless Area Conservation analysis, "Roads have long been recognized as the primary human-caused source of soil and water disturbances in forested environments." Roads of all kinds negatively affect aquatic and terrestrial ecosystems. A 2000 review of the ecological effects of roads underscored "the importance to conservation of avoiding construction of new roads in roadless or sparely roaded areas and of removal or restoration of existing roads to benefit both terrestrial and aquatic biota."

Former Northern Region Forester Hal Salwasser spoke at Montana State University in July, 1996 and claimed that the farther that you get from wilderness and roadless areas, the more damage you find. "Areas with the best ecological integrity tend to be associated with wilderness and roadless lands," Salwasser said. Initially viewed for Wilderness designation and recreation opportunities, roadless areas are gaining acknowledgement for their ecological importance for biodiversity, clean water, fisheries, and high quality wildlife habitat. Roadless areas are ecological strongholds—large blocks of land sufficiently intact and ecologically significant.

> *"The Northern Rockies is the only area in the country which still retains all of the wildlife species present when Lewis and Clark passed through in the early nineteenth century."*

The Scientific Assessment for the Interior Columbia Basin Ecosystem Management Project (ICBEMP), a joint USFS—Bureau of Land Management (BLM) proposal, has found that roadless areas are in far better ecological condition than roaded, heavily-managed portions of public lands. The Highlighted Scientific Findings of the ICBEMP examines ecological integrity and determines that "[a] system with high integrity functions properly because it has all its parts and processes intact. Such a system rebounds faster after wildfire, floods, road building, and other disturbances." Unroaded areas on the National Forests have more parts and processes intact than roaded areas on public land. The scientific findings also indicate, "in general, the more a system has been altered, the lower its integrity . . . [and] only 16% of the entire [Interior Columbia] basin is rated as having high ecological integrity."

Roadless areas are important for maintaining clean water and high quality fish habitat. Scientists have determined that roadless areas greater than 1,000 acres are ecologically important for trout conservation. . . .

Roadless areas are also the building blocks for conservation biology. Conservation biology is the applied science of maintaining the earth's biological diversity. A 2001 study highlights "the contribution that IRAs [Inventoried Roadless Areas] could make toward building a representative network of conservation reserves in the United States." According to conservation biologists, our propensity to split habitats into increasingly smaller parcels, via road building, clearcutting, etc., isolates various wildlife populations and leads to habitat fragmentation. Using conservation biology principles as a basis, several scientists argue that a system of core reserves is essential to restore natural ecosystem structure and function throughout the region. Their article notes that roadless lands can serve as starting points for building an expanded nature reserve network. This type of core reserve design is possible because there are large expanses of roadless land remaining. Approximately 63% of the Forest Service lands in the Northern Rockies remain in a roadless condition. . . .

The Northern Rockies is the only area in the country which still retains all of the wildlife species present when Lewis and Clark passed through in the early nineteenth century. This is largely due to the presence of high quality habitat in Wilderness and Inventoried Roadless Areas. More than 55% of Threatened and Endangered Species and 65% of Forest Service sensitive species are directly or indirectly affected by inventoried roadless areas. Roadless areas are ecologically important for maintenance of our fish and wildlife species, our clean water, and our forested scenery.

Economic Importance

Roadless areas are economically important to local and regional communities. . . .

Many regional economists argue that the protection of the remaining roadless areas is essential to our landscape-focussed local economy. Recent economic trends indicate that the growth of small businesses and tourism related to landscape amenities such as vast tracks of roadless lands are becoming much more important to thriving local economies than extractive industry.

The roles of extractive industry in the region, in fact, have declined significantly in the last few decades. The USFS's Status Report for the Interior Columbia Basin concludes, "Natural resource production plays a relatively small role in today's regional economy: just 4 percent of the total area's employment depends directly on timber, grazing, and mining." There has been a significant decline in timber logged from public lands. "Timber harvest in the Basin currently accounts for 10 percent of total United States harvest, down from 17 percent since 1986. . . ." This projected trend indicates the West's decreasing dependence on extractive industry for local and regional economies.

Roadless areas, in particular, are highlighted as important economic resources. The Forest Service's Status Report states, "The [Interior Columbia River] Basin's abundant unroaded areas are an irreplaceable national resource. . . . Landscape appearance and scenery are also important environmentally based amenities, not just as settings for recreation, but as components of the Basin's image both to residents and non-residents." This environmentally based amenity is supposed to continue to be an important part of the Basin's economy. "The existence of unroaded areas is a highly valued condition on FS- and BLM-administered lands in the Basin today. Projections indicate that it will continue to be so in the year 2045. . . ." Two economists estimated that the 42 million acres of roadless lands on National Forests in the 48 conterminous states can be expected to provide almost $600 million in recreation benefits annually, more than $280 million in passive use values, and nearly 24,000 jobs. Although Forest Service scientists and economists are beginning to understand the importance of roadless areas to the Northern Rockies, these areas remain threatened by the Bush Administration's Roadless Rule. The economics of roadless area preservation will be key to ensuring their protection.

The environmental-based amenity of roadless lands for local communities is not the only economic factor that needs to be considered. Roadless areas also curb federal spending because they retain their natural functions and provide quality wildlife and fisheries habitat. Because roadless areas are generally ecologically intact, the Forest Service does not need to conduct extensive restoration projects. These projects, funded by our tax dollars, are required to clean our water, replant forests, and restore wildlife habitat. The high cost of developing projects in roadless areas, and the additional costs of Endangered Species Act protection, stream restoration, and conservation planning, is an unnecessary tax burden on the public.

An essential part of protecting biodiversity in the Northern Rockies depends on retaining our remaining roadless lands. Over 440,000 acres have been developed since the Forest planning process. This figure underestimates the total loss due to poor Forest Service monitoring. Whether by directive or law, it is critical that all of the remaining roadless areas in the Northern Rockies receive full protection.

13

Sustainable Forest Management Will Ensure the Future Well-Being of Humanity

Richard W. Guldin and H. Fred Kaiser

Richard W. Guldin is the director of science policy, planning, inventory, and information for the U.S. Department of Agriculture Forest Service's research and development division. H. Fred Kaiser is an economist for the USDA Forest Service.

Forest managers have to consider the desires of hikers, loggers, hunters, scientists, and environmentalists as well as the citizens who rely on cheap wood and paper products. Over the past century, the concept of sustainable development, or managing the forest to meet current needs while making sure that future generations will also be able to meet their needs, has evolved to deal with these often conflicting desires. Managers wishing to create sustainable forests must harvest, plant, and, in some cases, preserve trees in order to maintain healthy natural environments, maximize the economic value of forest resources, and satisfy the needs of recreation users. While it is difficult and challenging to accomplish all of these tasks, it is also vital to protect and sustain forests and their resources.

A new century has dawned. With it has come increased demand for goods, services, and amenities from the private

Richard W. Guldin and H. Fred Kaiser, "National Report on Sustainable Forests—2003," U.S. Department of Agriculture, www.fs.fed.us, 2003.

and public forests of the United States. Increasing population and increasing urban centers are creating demands on our forests that were not envisioned a century ago. Today, 270 percent more U.S. citizens are being supported by essentially the same forest land area—749 million acres—as existed in 1900. Certainly we are closer to the limits of our forests' capability to provide the things people want today than we were in 1900. . . .

> *"We are still in the process of debating and defining the meanings of sustainability."*

While many ideas about sustainability have been put forward during the last two decades, almost all are consistent with the basic concept of sustainable development found in the 1987 Brundtland Commission Report [written by the World Commission on Environment and Development (WCED)]. The Brundtland Commission defined sustainable development as—

> . . . development that meets the needs of the present without compromising the ability of future generations to meet their own needs.

The concept of sustainable development links the environment, society, and the economy. These three basic components or spheres of sustainable development are often stated as three interdependent goals of environmental protection, social well-being, and economic prosperity. The essential idea is that environmental social, and economic issues and values must be integrated into our decision making and actions, while accounting for future as well as present needs. In all decisions, the long-term effects on resources and capital, as well as the capacity for the future creation of benefits, should be considered. In its 1999 report, *Our Common Journey: A Transition toward Sustainability*, the National Research Council's Board on Sustainable Development described sustainable development as "the reconciliation of society's developmental goals with its environmental limits over the long term." The board also noted that "any successful quest for sustainability will necessarily be a collective, uncertain, and adaptive endeavor in which society's discovering of where it wants to go and how it might try to get there will be inextricably intertwined."

Thus, this report presumes that sustainability should be viewed as more of a journey than a destination. It is not a fixed target, and the pathway to sustainability may involve a range of acceptable outcomes, as well as a range of feasible courses to reaching those outcomes determined by carefully weighing environmental, social, and economic criteria. The Brundtland Commission describes the journey this way: ". . . in the end, sustainable development is not a fixed state of harmony, but rather a process of change in which the exploitation of resources, the direction of investments, the orientation of technological development, and institutional change are made consistent with future as well as present needs."

> *"Because we cannot predict what they will value most, future citizens should not be denied the opportunity to make their own choices."*

Recognizing that sustainability is a global concern and a common goal for human development, the United States and 177 other nations of the world came together at the Rio Earth Summit in 1992, and agreed to take concrete steps to advance sustainable development. Forest issues were a major focus of discussion at the Earth Summit, and sustainable forest management was recognized as a key part of the global goal of sustainable development. A Statement of Forest Principles, declaring the importance of managing all forests in a sustainable manner, was adopted as the first global agreement on forests. In the United States, during the decade following the Earth Summit, various national dialogs about sustainable development and sustainable forest management were initiated. . . . These dialogs resulted in the adoption of goals and policy recommendations for the United States.

At the 2002 World Summit on Sustainable Development (WSSD), the United States and other nations reaffirmed their commitment to the Rio principles. . . . For example, the WSSD plan of implementation makes this statement regarding forests:

> Sustainable forest management . . . is essential to achieving sustainable development and is a critical means to eradicate poverty, significantly re-

> duce deforestation and halt the loss of forest biodiversity and land and resource degradation, and improve food security and access to safe drinking water and affordable energy; highlights the multiple benefits of both natural and planted forests and trees; and contributes to the well-being of the planet and humanity.

Defining Sustainable Forest Management

In the book *Forest Sustainability: the History, the Challenge, the Promise*, Donald Floyd observes that—

> . . . trying to define sustainability and sustainable forestry is like trying to define "justice" or "democracy." There are many definitions and some consensus, but agreement over the specifics is elusive. If sustainability cannot be specifically defined, does that mean it is of little value? Foresters know there are many useful yet ambiguous terms, like "multiple use," "forest health" and "ecosystem." We come to grips with any new idea through discussion and debate, and we are still in the process of debating and defining the meanings of sustainability.

The terms *forest sustainability* and *sustainable forest management* are sometimes used interchangeably, and refer to the same basic concept. The concept has been given specific meaning through the development of criteria and indicators for sustainable forest management. The *Dictionary of Forestry* offers this description of forest sustainability:

> . . . the capacity of forests, ranging from stands to ecoregions, to maintain their health, productivity, diversity, and overall integrity, in the long run, in the context of human activity and use.

The *Dictionary of Forestry* also states that sustainable forest management is an evolving concept that has several definitions. . . .

1. The practice of meeting the forest resources needs . . . of the present without compromising the similar capability of future generations—note sustainable forest management involves practicing a land stewardship ethic that integrates the reforestation, managing, growing, nurturing, and harvesting of

trees for useful products with the conservation of soil, air and water quality, wildlife and fish habitat, and aesthetics.

2. The stewardship and use of forests and forest lands in a way, and at a rate, that maintains their biodiversity, productivity, regeneration capacity, vitality, and potential to fulfill, now and in the future, relevant ecological, economic, and social functions at local, national, and global levels, and that does not cause damage to other ecosystems—note criteria for sustainable forestry include (a) conservation of biological diversity, (b) maintenance of productive capacity of forest ecosystems, (c) maintenance of forest ecosystem health and vitality, (d) conservation and maintenance of soil and water resources, (e) maintenance of forest contribution to global carbon cycles, (f) maintenance and enhancement of long-term multiple socioeconomic benefits to meet the needs of societies, and (g) legal, institutional, and economic framework for forest conservation and sustainable management.

The Society of American Foresters adopted the following statement defining the concept of sustainable forest management:

> Sustainability as applied to forestry is the enhancement of human well-being by using, developing, and protecting resources at a rate and in a manner that enables people to meet their current needs while also providing future generations with the means to meet their needs as well; it requires simultaneously meeting environmental, economic, and community aspirations. . . .

The *Sourcebook on Criteria and Indicators of Forest Sustainability in the Northeastern Area* sums up the key features of most definitions in this statement about forest sustainability:

> . . . it involves the continued existence and use of forests to meet human physical, economic, and social needs; the desire to preserve the health of forest ecosystems in perpetuity; and the ethical choice of preserving options for future generations while meeting the needs of the present.

The concept of sustainable forest management is related to but different in significant ways from an earlier concept of sustained yield—the amount of wood that a forest can produce on a continual basis. The concept of sustained yield, dating back to the Middle Ages in Europe, was brought to the United States in the late 1800s by early forestry leaders such as Bernhard Fernow and Gifford Pinchot [both of whom worked in the first government forestry bureaus]. It was expanded over time to include the perpetual production of other forest outputs in addition to timber supply, including water, recreation, fish and wildlife, and livestock forage—the expanded concept is often referred to as the "multiple-use sustained-yield" principle. This principle was enshrined in law in 1960 for national forests. The concept of sustainable forest management, however, includes managing the forest for more than outputs; it focuses on maintaining processes and seeking to sustain communities, economies, and all the elements of a forest.

For Future Generations

Sustainable forest management also denotes maintaining capacities for future generations to meet their needs. Because we cannot predict what they will value most, future citizens should not be denied the opportunity to make their own choices. We need to ensure that the environmental, social, and economic systems that provide what people value from forests endure so that future generations can enjoy the benefits that they choose to value.

> *"Americans value the availability of resources for posterity more than either current environmental or economic welfare."*

One of the keys to sustainability is having a suite of values that recognizes the interrelationships among all three spheres. For example, if the society values both economic growth and the environmental qualities required to sustain the economy, then it is more likely to develop the traditions and institutions necessary for sustainability. In the United States, there are signs that citizens care about the environment. [Researcher Michael] Tarrent et al. (2003) found that the public "favors a balance of environmental protection and economic development in public and private forests, but with a very strong tilt in favor of the environment." [Brian] Czech [of the U.S. Fish and Wildlife Service] and Krausman (1999) found that Americans value the availability of resources for posterity more than either current environmental or economic welfare. As expressed in survey responses, Americans have developed key aspects of a long-term social perspective in favor of protecting the environmental and economic spheres of sustainability.

Sustaining the full range of services and benefits (environmental, social, and economic) that people desire from forests will usually require a diverse mosaic of ownerships, forest conditions, and capacities across the landscape, as well as a variety of management emphases. Though our society has some core shared goals for what forest management should sustain . . . specific resource management objectives will still vary among different types of landowners and among other stakeholders. Given the necessary information and incentives, the various landowners can manage their forests in light of their individual, private objectives and their shared community goals, while providing a mix of different products, services, and other benefits that, in combination, meet the broad range of objectives that society has for forests.

Organizations to Contact

The editors have compiled the following list of organizations concerned with issues debated in this book. The descriptions are derived from materials provided by the organizations. All have publications or information available for interested readers. The list was compiled on the date of publication of the present volume; the information provided here may change. Be aware that many organizations take several weeks or longer to respond to inquiries, so allow as much time as possible.

Aldo Leopold Wilderness Research Institute
PO Box 8-89, Missoula, MT 59807
(406) 542-9190
e-mail: RMRS_Leopold_Institute@fs.fed.us
Web site: http://leopold.wilderness.net

The Aldo Leopold Wilderness Research Institute is the only federal research group in the United States dedicated to the development and dissemination of the knowledge needed to improve management of wilderness, parks, and protected areas. The institute, established in 1993 by the U.S. Forest Service, provides a national center for scientists from different disciplines and backgrounds to address the wilderness research needs of land management agencies and organizations. The institute Web site lists over five hundred downloadable publications that cover a wide array of wilderness topics.

American Lands Alliance (ALA)
726 Seventh St. SE, Washington, DC 20003
(202) 547-9400 • fax: (202) 547-9213
e-mail: ldix@americanlands.org • Web site: www.americanlands.org

The American Lands Alliance is an environmental organization that represents grassroots activists in Washington, D.C., in their efforts to protect the ancient forests of the Pacific Northwest. Founded in 1990, the ALA also represents citizens nationwide who are working to protect wildlife and wild places and to develop effective national strategies to preserve these places in perpetuity. Numerous environmental reports and issues of the newsletter *Landscope* are available on the group's Web site.

American Tree Farm System (ATFS)
c/o American Forest Foundation
1111 Nineteenth St. NW, Suite 780, Washington, DC 20036
(202) 463-2462 • fax: (202) 463-2461
e-mail: info@treefarmsystem.org • Web site: www.treefarmsystem.org

The American Tree Farm System promotes growing and harvesting trees on private lands and increasing public understanding of all benefits of productive forestry. The ATFS is committed to sustaining forests, watershed, and healthy habitats through the private stewardship of forests.

The organization publishes *Tree Farmer Magazine*, a landowner's guide to forest management.

American Wildlands
40 East Main St., Suite 2, PO Box 6669, Bozeman, MT 59771
(406) 586-8175 • fax: (406) 586-8242
e-mail: info@wildlands.org • Web site: www.wildlands.org

American Wildlands is a regional conservation organization that advocates for the protection and restoration of the U.S. northern Rocky Mountain region. Using science and state-of-the-art computer mapping, American Wildlands identifies and prioritizes the wildlands, waters, and species habitats most in need of conservation. The group works with political leaders to shape policies and projects to protect the wilderness for future generations.

Competitive Enterprise Institute (CEI)
1001 Connecticut Ave. NW, Suite 1250, Washington, DC 20036
(202) 331-1010 • fax: (202) 331-0640
e-mail: info@cei.org • Web site: www.cei.org

CEI encourages the use of the free market and private property rights to protect the environment. It advocates removing governmental regulatory barriers and establishing a system in which the private sector would be responsible for the environment. CEI's publications include the monthly newsletter *CEI Update* and editorials in its On Point series, such as "Property Owners Deserve Equal Access to Justice."

Environmental Defense Fund (EDF)
257 Park Ave. South, New York, NY 10010
(212) 505-2100 • fax: (212) 505-0892
e-mail: members@environmentaldefense.org • Web site: www.edf.org

The fund is a public interest organization of lawyers, scientists, and economists dedicated to the protection and improvement of environmental quality and public health. It publishes brochures, fact sheets, and the bimonthly *EDF Letter.*

Forest Service Employees for Environmental Ethics (FSEEE)
PO Box 11615, Eugene, OR 97440
(541) 484-2692 • fax: (541) 484-3004
e-mail: fseee@fseee.org • Web site: www.fseee.org

The FSEEE is made up of thousands of concerned citizens; present, former, and retired Forest Service employees; other government resource managers; and activists working to change the U.S. Forest Service's land management philosophy. FSEEE believes that the land is a public trust to be passed with reverence from generation to generation. The group publishes various environmental reports and *Forest Magazine,* which covers topics such as forest recreation, clean water, wildlife sanctuaries, and wilderness.

Foundation for Research on Economics and the Environment (FREE)
945 Technology Blvd., Suite 101F, Bozeman, MT 59718
(406) 585-1776 • fax: (406) 585-3000
e-mail: free@mcn.net • Web site: www.free-eco.org

FREE is a research and education foundation committed to freedom, environmental quality, and economic progress. It works to reform environmental policy that upholds the principles of private property rights, the free market, and the rule of law. FREE publishes the quarterly newsletter *FREE Perspectives on Economics and the Environment* and produces a biweekly syndicated op-ed column.

Greenpeace USA
702 H St. NW, Suite 300, Washington, DC 20001
(202) 462-1177 • fax: (202) 462-4507
e-mail: greenpeace.usa@wdc.greenpeace.org
Web site: www.greenpeace.org

Greenpeace has been campaigning against environmental degradation since 1971. Greenpeace exists to expose environmental criminals and to challenge government and corporations when they fail to live up to their mandate to safeguard the environment and the future. The organization uses research, lobbying, and diplomacy as well as high-profile, nonviolent conflict to pursue its goals. Greenpeace publishes press releases and detailed environmental reports on its Web site.

Greenspirit
(604) 221-1990
Web site: www.greenspirit.com

Greenspirit is an organization run by Greenpeace founder Patrick Moore. Greenspirit believes that large-scale logging can benefit the environment by replacing fossil fuels with wood as an energy source. It also advocates replacing steel, concrete, and plastic materials with wood where possible and believes that some agricultural fields that produce food should be converted to tree farms.

Heritage Foundation
214 Massachusetts Ave. NE, Washington, DC 20002
(800) 544-4843 • fax: (202) 544-2260
e-mail: pubs@heritage.org • Web site: www.heritage.org

The Heritage Foundation is a conservative think tank that supports the principles of free enterprise and limited government in environmental matters. Its many publications include the following position papers: "Can No One Stop the EPA?" "How to Talk About Property Rights: Why Protecting Property Rights Benefits All Americans," and "How to Help the Environment Without Destroying Jobs." The foundation publishes various reports on its Web site and *Policy Wire*, a weekly digest available by e-mail.

National Audubon Society
700 Broadway, New York, NY 10003
(212) 979-3000 • fax: (212) 979-3188
e-mail: education@audubon.org • Web site: www.audubon.org

Audubon's mission is to conserve and restore natural ecosystems, focusing on birds, other wildlife, and their habitats for the benefit of humanity and the earth's biological diversity. Its national network of community-based nature centers provides scientific and educational programs and advocates on behalf of areas sustaining important bird populations. The society publishes *Audubon* magazine, featuring articles about wildlife and the environment.

National Network of Forest Practitioners (NNFP)
National Community Forestry Center
305 Main St., Providence, RI 02903
(401) 273-6507 • fax: (401) 273-6508
e-mail: thomas@nnfp.org • Web site: www.nnfp.org

The National Network of Forest Practitioners is an alliance of rural people working to build a forest economy that is ecologically sound and socially just. The NNFP is one of the leading community forestry organizations in the United States that helps people solve problems, experiment with new approaches, work with unconventional partners, and compete in the marketplace. The group advocates for a change in forestry and forest conservation, focusing on the long-term well-being of the environment, forest communities, and forest workers.

Natural Resources Defense Council (NRDC)
40 West Twentieth St., New York, NY 10011
(212) 727-2700 • fax: (212) 727-1773
e-mail: nrdcinfo@nrdc.org • Web site: www.nrdc.org

The Natural Resources Defense Council is an environmental organization with more than 1 million members and online activists working to protect the planet's wildlife and natural resources such as air, land, and water. The group's mission is to ensure a safe and healthy environment for all living things. The NRDC publishes *Nature's Choice*, a bulletin of environmental campaigns and victories, and *OnEarth* magazine which explores politics, nature, wildlife, science, and environmental threats.

Property and Environment Research Center (PERC)
502 South Nineteenth Ave., Suite 211, Bozeman, MT 59718-6872
(406) 587-9591 • fax: (406) 586-7555
e-mail: perc@perc.org • Web site: www.perc.org

PERC is a research and education foundation that focuses on environmental and natural resource issues. It emphasizes the advantages of free markets and the importance of private property rights in environmental protection. PERC's publications include the monthly *PERC Reports* and papers in the PERC Policy series such as "The Common Law: How It Protects the Environment."

Religious Campaign for Forest Conservation (RCFC)
409 Mendocino Ave., Suite A, Santa Rosa, CA 95401
(707) 573-3162
e-mail: forest@creationethics.org • Web site: http://creationethics.org

The Religious Campaign for Forest Conservation is a coalition of churches, synagogues, and other religious organizations that believe forest and wilderness conservation is a religious issue. The RCFC believes that the spiritual value of forests is far greater than the economic value that is assigned to them.

Sierra Club
85 Second St., 2nd Floor, San Francisco, CA 94105-3441
(415) 977-5500 • fax: (415) 977-5799
e-mail: information@sierraclub.org • Web site: www.sierraclub.org

The Sierra Club is a nonprofit public interest organization that promotes conservation of the natural environment by influencing public policy decisions—legislative, administrative, legal, and electoral. It publishes *Sierra* magazine as well as dozens of books on the environment.

Society of American Foresters (SAF)
5400 Grosvenor Ln., Bethesda, MD 20814
(301) 897-8720 • fax: (301) 897-3690
e-mail: safweb@safnet.org • Web site: www.safnet.org

The Society of American Foresters is the national scientific and educational organization representing the forestry profession in the United States. The largest professional society for foresters in the world, the SAF's mission is to advance the science, education, technology, and practice of forestry; to enhance the competency of its members; and to use the knowledge, skills, and conservation ethic of the profession to ensure the continued health and use of forest ecosystems and the present and future availability of forest resources to benefit society.

USDA Forest Service
1400 Independence Ave. SW, Washington, DC 20250-0003
(202) 205-3333
Web site: www.fs.fed.us

The U.S. Department of Agriculture Forest Service is a federal agency that manages public lands in national forests and grasslands. Congress established the Forest Service in 1905 to provide quality water and timber to the nation. Over the years, Forest Service mandates have grown to include managing national forests for multiple uses and benefits and for the sustained yield of renewable resources such as water, forage, wildlife, wood, and recreation.

The Wilderness Institute
College of Forestry and Conservation
University of Montana, Missoula, MT 59812
(406) 243-5361
e-mail: wi@forestry.umt.edu
Web site: www.forestry.umt.edu/research/MFCES/programs/wi

Housed within the University of Montana's College of Forestry and Conservation, the Wilderness Institute provides students, agencies, and the public with information, education, and an understanding of the issues and social and ecological values of wilderness. The Wilderness Institute was created in 1975 by a group of nineteen scientists, educators, land agency personnel, and leading conservationists.

Bibliography

Books

Joni Adamson, Mei Mei Evans, and Rachel Stein, eds. *The Environmental Justice Reader: Politics, Poetics, & Pedagogy.* Tucson: University of Arizona Press, 2002.

Michael Anderson *Idaho's Vanishing Wild Lands: A Status Report on Roadless Areas in Idaho's National Forests.* Washington, DC: Wilderness Society, 1997.

Karen Arabas and Joe Bowersox, eds. *Forest Futures: Science, Politics, and Policy for the Next Century.* Lanham, MD: Rowman & Littlefield, 2004.

Robert Bott *Learning from the Forest: A Fifty-Year Journey in Sustainable Forest Management.* Calgary, AB: Fifth House, 2003.

Robert Burton, ed. *Nature's Last Strongholds.* New York: Oxford University Press, 1991.

Thomas D. Clark *The Greening of the South: The Recovery of Land and Forest.* Lexington: University Press of Kentucky, 2004.

Carol J. Pierce Colfer and Yvonne Byron, eds. *People Managing Forests: The Links Between Human Well-Being and Sustainability.* Washington, DC: Resources for the Future, 2001.

Kathie Durbin *Tongass: Pulp Politics and the Fight for the Alaska Rain Forest.* Corvallis: Oregon State University Press, 1999.

Felipe Fernández-Armesto *Civilizations: Culture, Ambition, and the Transformation of Nature.* New York: Free Press, 2001.

Frank Friedman *Practical Guide to Environmental Management.* Washington, DC: Environmental Law Institute, 1995.

Elizabeth Grossman *Adventuring Along the Lewis and Clark Trail: Missouri, Illinois, Iowa, Nebraska, South Dakota, North Dakota, Montana, Idaho, Oregon, Washington.* San Francisco: Sierra Club, 2003.

Lesley Head *Cultural Landscapes and Environmental Change.* London: Arnold, 2000.

John C. Hendee, George H. Stankey, and Robert C. Lucas *Wilderness Management.* Golden, CO: North American, 1990.

J.P. Kimmins — *Forest Ecology: A Foundation for Sustainable Management.* Upper Saddle River, NJ: Prentice-Hall, 1997.

Nancy Langston — *Forest Dreams, Forest Nightmares: The Paradox of Old Growth in the Inland West.* Seattle: University of Washington Press, 1995.

Aldo Leopold — *A Sand County Almanac.* New York: Oxford University Press, 1987.

Elizabeth May — *At the Cutting Edge: The Crisis in Canada's Forests.* San Francisco: Sierra Club, 1998.

Norman Myers and Jennifer Kent — *Perverse Subsidies: How Tax Dollars Can Undercut the Environment and the Economy.* Covelo, CA: Island Press, 2001.

John Muir — *The American Wilderness.* New York: Barnes & Noble, 1993.

John Muir — *The Mountains of California.* New York: Century, 1894.

National Research Council — *Forested Lands in Perspective: Prospects and Opportunities for Sustainable Management of America's Nonfederal Forests.* Washington, DC: National Academy, 1998.

Bob R. O'Brien — *Our National Parks and the Search for Sustainability.* Austin: University of Texas Press, 1999.

Rosemary O'Leary — *Managing for the Environment: Understanding the Legal, Organizational, and Policy Challenges.* San Francisco: Jossey-Bass, 1999.

Carl Pope and Paul Rauber — *Strategic Ignorance: Why the Bush Administration Is Recklessly Destroying a Century of Environmental Progress.* San Francisco: Sierra Club, 2004.

K.A. Soderberg — *People of the Tongass: Alaska Forestry Under Attack.* Bellevue, WA: Free Enterprise, 1988.

Bill Willers — *Unmanaged Landscapes: Voices for Untamed Nature.* Washington, DC: Island Press, 1999.

Periodicals

H. Michael Anderson — "Reshaping National Forest Policy," *Issues in Science and Technology*, Fall 1999.

Peter Annin — "Saving the Tall Timber," *Newsweek*, September 17, 1999.

W.H. Banzhaf — "Commentary: We Stand for Sustainability," *Journal of Forestry*, 2001.

Gary Bryner — "Balancing Preservation and Logging: Public Lands Policy in British Columbia and the Western United States," *Policy Studies Journal*, Summer 1999.

George Busenberg	"Wildfire Management in the United States: The Evolution of a Policy Failure," *Review of Policy Research*, March 2004.
Keith Easthouse	"Out of Control," *Forest Magazine*, May/June 2000.
Jennifer Hattam	"Highway Robbery: Make-Believe Roads Threaten Real Wilderness," *Sierra*, July/August, 2003.
Tony Juniper and Sarah Tyack	"A Policy Imperative: Save and Plant Trees," *Ecologist*, March/April 1999.
Paul R. Krausman and Brian Czech	"Wildlife Management Activities in Wilderness Areas in the Southwestern United States," *Wildlife Society Bulletin*, Fall 2000.
Margaret Kriz	"Fighting Fire with Logging," *National Journal*, July 13, 2002.
Jessie Mangaliman	"New Rules to Triple Amount of Logging Allowed in California's Sierra Nevada," *San Jose Mercury News*, January 23, 2004.
Robert H. Nelson	"Scorched-Earth Policies," *Wall Street Journal*, November 3, 2003.
Dan Oko and Ilan Kayatsky	"Fight Fire with Logging?" *Mother Jones*, August 1, 2002.
Deborah Schoch	"Faux Forests? Pine Plantations Replacing Native Hardwoods in the South," *Los Angeles Times*, July 8, 2002.
Roger A. Sedjo	"Does the Forest Service Have a Future?" *Regulation*, Winter 2000.
Robert J. Smith	"A New Beginning for Our Forests," *San Diego Union-Tribune*, December 9, 2003.
Toddi A. Steelman	"Elite and Participatory Policymaking: Finding Balance in a Case of National Forest Planning," *Policy Studies Journal*, Spring 2000.
Brendon Swedlow	"Scientists, Judges, and Spotted Owls: Policymakers in the Pacific Northwest," *Duke Environmental Law & Policy Forum*, Spring 2003.
William Wallace	"Helping Western Forests Heal," *Nature*, November 9, 2000.
David N. Wear and John G. Greis	"Southern Forest Resource Assessment," USDA Forest Service, www.srs.fs.usda.gov/sustain. October 11, 2003.
Sandra B. Zellmer	"The Roadless Area Controversy: Past, Present, and Future," *Rocky Mountain Mineral Law Institute*, 2002.

Index